True Crime Stories

12 Shocking True Crime Murder Cases

True Crime Anthology Vol.5

By
Jack Rosewood

Copyright © 2016 by LAK Publishing

ALL RIGHTS RESERVED

No part of this book may be reproduced, stored in a retrieval system, or transmitted in any form or by any means, electronic, mechanical, photocopying, recording, scanning, or otherwise, without the prior written permission of the publisher.

ISBN-13: 978-1542336000

DISCLAIMER:

This crime anthology biography includes quotes from those closely involved in the twelve cases examined, and it is not the author's intention to defame or intentionally hurt anyone involved. The interpretation of the events leading up to these crimes are the author's as a result of researching the true crime murders. Any comments made about the psychopathic or sociopathic behavior of criminals involved in any of these cases are the sole opinion and responsibility of the person quoted.

Free Bonus!

**Get two free books when you sign up to my VIP newsletter
at** www.jackrosewood.com
**150 interesting trivia about serial killers
and the story of serial killer Herbert Mullin.**

Contents

Introduction 1

CHAPTER 1: The Murder of Susan Schwarz 4

    The Queen of Hearts 5

    The Murder 6

    The Investigation 9

    It's All in the Cards 11

    The Aftermath 15

CHAPTER 2: Victor Licata and "Reefer Madness" 16

    A Brutal Axe Murder 18

    A Bloodbath Uncovered 19

    The Licata Killings, Yellow Journalism, and the Crusade against Marijuana 21

    Victor Licata's Mental Health 22

CHAPTER 3: The Scott Peterson Murder Trial 24

    Two Lives Intersect 25

    The Disappearance of Laci Peterson 28

    Suspicious Scott 31

    The Discovery of Laci's Body 34

    The Arrest and Trial of Scott Peterson 36

The Aftermath 41

CHAPTER 4: The Trial of Football Superstar Rae Carruth 43

Against the Odds 44

Rae Carruth Makes the Bigtime... 45

The Hit on Cherica Adams.. 47

Running for His Life 51

The Trial 52

CHAPTER 5: The Strange and Fascinating Life of Jack Kevorkian 54

A Student of Death 55

The Doctor of Death in Action 60

Legal Problems for the Doctor of Death...................................... 62

Jack Kevorkian's Influence on America 66

CHAPTER 6: The Saga of the Menendez Brothers 67

The American Dream 68

Erik and Lyle Menendez 70

Massacre at the Menendez Home 72

Living Large 75

The Arrest and Trial of the Menendez Brothers 76

CHAPTER 7: The Murder of the Wilson Family 81

A Gothic Mystery... 82

Every Man for Himself 87

The Murder Trials of David Anderson and Alex Baranyi............ 89

CHAPTER 8: The Robert Blake Murder Trial 92

    Bonnie Lee Bakley 93

    The Murder 94

    Baretta Goes on Trial 96

CHAPTER 9: The Cold Case Murder of Helen Sullivan 100

    A Horrible Discovery 102

    A Cold Case Solved: Postmortem 103

CHAPTER 10: A Guilty Conscience and the Cold Murder Case of Frederick Hart 107

    A Senseless Murder 107

    A Troubled Life 109

    The Guilty Plea 111

CHAPTER 11: The Murder of Dominique Dunne 113

    A Privileged Life 113

    A Promising Life Cut Short 115

    The Trial of John Sweeney 117

CHAPTER 12: Eva Dugan and the Politics of Death 119

    A Wild Life 120

    Another Mysterious Disappearance.................................... 122

    An Execution that Changed the Law 124

Conclusion..126

Introduction

Today, it seems that we cannot avoid crime. We hear about it in the news, especially around election time, and unfortunately many of us have been victims of crime. In some places, it has become so much a part of our lives that at times we have become oblivious and desensitized to it.

Unfortunately, crime is here to stay.

With so much crime all around us, we often do not take the time to learn about the origins of specific crimes or how they were resolved.

In the following book, you will read the details about how twelve high-profile crimes began and ultimately how they were resolved. You will find the motives of some of these criminals and killers as intriguing as they are disturbing. You may even find yourself empathizing with some of them!

You will follow along with homicide detectives who solve cases through hard work, despite a lack of forensic evidence. You will read how cold case detectives solved the thirty-year-old murder mystery of Susan Schwarz and how Scott Peterson was convicted of the murder of his wife without much physical evidence.

Advances in forensic science also helped cold case detectives solve the murder of Helen Sullivan in Long Beach, California. After forty years, it was a murder that was long forgotten by most people other than the Sullivan family and the dedicated detectives who eventually solved the case.

Sometimes, though, neither good police work nor scientific advances can solve a cold case. In these cases, such as the murder of Ricky Hart, a little luck and the guilty conscience of a troubled soul helped solve the mystery.

Many of us are deeply intrigued with situations where the rich and famous run afoul of the law. In some ways, it is like watching a train wreck, while at the same time we like to know, whether we admit it or not, that the rich and famous are just like the rest of us with the same problems and flaws. The high-profile murder trial of actor Robert Blake was one such case that is profiled in this book. The high-profile life of Jack Kevorkian is also depicted here, along with the tragic murder of heiress and actress Dominque Dunne.

Sometimes the rich and the famous think that their money and fame entitles them to a different set of rules. Cases of entitlement leading to murder are rare, but two notable cases are profiled in this book. Entitled killers sometimes pay others to eliminate a perceived obstacle through murder, like former NFL star Rae Carruth, or they kill to obtain a fortune, such as Erik and Lyle Menendez.

Finally, since murder is an essentially unpredictable act, no book about astonishing crime cases would be complete without some bizarre examples. Victor Lacata's axe murder of his family surely fits the bill of bizarre, but the subsequent media circus and attempts by government officials to correlate the murders to marijuana use made the case even stranger. Then there are the seemingly senseless murders, such as the Wilson family murder, where no rational motive can be found and the identity of the perpetrators is almost as surprising as the crime itself.

So open the pages of this book and immerse yourself into twelve of the most astonishing cases in crime history.

CHAPTER 1:
The Murder of Susan Schwarz

Throughout world history, playing cards and crime have seemed to go together. Although the use of cards began as an innocuous past time, it evolved over the centuries to become one of the favorite vocations of criminals, conmen, and swindlers. In the United States in particular, cards have long been associated with those on the fringes of mainstream society.

Images of "wild west" saloons, where rough cowpokes play poker against each other while elaborately dressed "saloon girls" look on, have been etched into the American psyche. One only has to watch reruns of popular television shows, such as *Gunsmoke* and *Maverick*, to see the importance that cards played in the imagination of Americans.

But the reality was not far from the television depictions. In the late nineteenth century, when much of what is now the western United States was still unincorporated territory, gambling halls that doubled as brothels were a ubiquitous part of life on the frontier.

The American association of cards with crime continued long after the west was won.

When Las Vegas legalized gambling in 1931, a surge of entrepreneurs flocked to the desert town to open casinos. Among them were members of organized crime.

Although Las Vegas has since been sanitized and the influence of organized crime over its casinos mitigated, playing cards continue to be associated with crime.

In more recent years, interest in serial killers has led to a plethora of books being written, a number of documentaries being produced, and even sets of serial killer trading cards being made.

In the early 2000s, the Snohomish County Sherriff's Department in Washington State decided to take advantage of America's connection between crime and cards by producing a set of "cold case cards."

The Queen of Hearts

Taking a cue from the emerging popularity of serial killer trading cards, the Snohomish County Sherriff's Department decided to initiate a program in 2008 that would place the victims of their unsolved homicide cases onto trading cards. The cards were styled after traditional trading cards, but instead of placing the traditional figures in the middle of the card—jack, king, queen, etc.—they used a photo of a specific victim of a cold case murder.

Susan Schwarz, a 1979 murder victim, was designated the "queen of hearts" on the first edition of the cards.

Snohomish County authorities distributed the cards to area schools, businesses, and also handed them out at the station. Most importantly, they distributed the cards to county jails and state prisons throughout Washington. They clung to the hope that an inmate who saw Schwarz's card and was involved in her murder, or had information about her murder, would feel a sense of guilt and go to the authorities.

Or perhaps the inmate might be willing to talk in exchange for more privileges behind bars or a reduction of time.

Either way, the Snohomish County Sherriff's Department was desperate to solve the case and willing to use any method to capture Schwarz's killer.

In 2010, an inmate serving time in the Washington State Department of Corrections saw the card and went to the authorities with an interesting story!

The Murder

On the afternoon of October 22, 1979, twenty-six-year old Susan Schwarz was found by her live-in boyfriend, Bill Hassler, shot to death in her Lynnwood, Washington home. It was quickly revealed that Susan suffered a brutal death.

Her hands had been bound and the autopsy revealed that she had been shot three times in the head. Some items were missing from the home, which suggested a possible random burglary gone wrong, but there were other elements of the crime that seemed to contradict the random killer theory.

Although some items were missing from the home, other more valuable items were untouched, which led some of the initial investigators to believe that the scene was staged to look like a burglary.

Then there was the position of the body.

The fact that Susan was bound possibly suggested that she did in fact stumble upon a burglary, but then why did the killer shoot her once she was bound? Most burglars, even those who enter buildings armed, try to avoid violence by any measures. If they have to subdue a victim then they do so, but they rarely kill the victim. Most burglars are professional criminals who know that a burglary-murder can result in the death penalty in states with capital punishment, like Washington. Burglars also tend to know what they are looking for and where to find it. Therefore, homes hit by seasoned burglars tend to be less ransacked than the normal person would think. They do not waste time in rooms where valuables are not usually kept and when in bedrooms, which is where most valuables are found, they begin with the bottom drawer and work their way up.

This information began to lead Snohomish County investigators to believe that Susan knew her killer. The suspicion was confirmed in many of their minds when they saw that her head was covered by a towel. Oftentimes, when a murder victim is found with his or her head covered, the perpetrator turns out to be someone who knew the victim. It as if the killer covers the face of the victim out of either a sense of remorse or fear.

The investigators began with a reasonable amount of evidence, but finding suspects proved to be easier said than done.

Who would want to kill Susan Schwarz?

Some killers need no motive to take another human's life, but in most cases there is a clear motive: revenge, greed, and lust are three of the most common reasons to kill. In Susan Schwarz's case, none of those three reasons seemed to apply early in the investigation. She had no known enemies, she was not wealthy, and the autopsy showed no signs of sexual assault. Because a motive for Susan's murder was not readily apparent, the Snohomish County investigators were forced to delve deeper into the young woman's background.

A background check revealed that Susan was not involved in drug use or criminal activity. In fact, Susan received nothing but praise from her employer and was fairly close to her family. She was known to be a good friend who was willing to help others out of trouble, no matter the situation. In particular, not long before she was murdered, Susan helped a friend move out of the home of her abusive husband and into a battered woman's shelter.

Susan was truly a person willing to help others; but did that helpful attitude get her killed?

The Investigation

The clues that the Snohomish County investigators initially picked up in the Susan Schwarz murder seemed to point in a number of different directions. But like most murder investigations, the person closest to the victim went to the top of the suspect list.

At the very beginning of the investigation, Bill Hassler looked like the perfect suspect. He was the boyfriend of the victim and was the person who found her body. Also, since he was Susan's live-in boyfriend, he had unlimited access to the crime scene. There was also the fact that Susan had not been raped and her head was covered after the homicide.

All of these facts seemed to point directly at Bill Hassler.

An investigation of Bill Hassler's background revealed that, like Susan, he was not involved in drugs or criminal activity. Susan's friends and family also told the police that Bill treated Susan well and that they had never seen any signs of abuse.

Although forensic science in 1979 was nowhere near the level that it is today, coroners could determine the time of death fairly accurately due to the level of rigor mortis of the body. The science clearly showed that Bill Hassler's alibi checked out and that he could not have murdered Susan.

With Hassler crossed off their suspect list, the Snohomish County investigators widened their search to include more of Susan's friends. The more they asked her friends who may have committed such a horrible crime, the more the name of Gregory Johnson kept coming up.

In 1979, Gregory Johnson was a twenty-six-year-old man with few prospects for a good future. He was a petty criminal with no real job skills who lived off the proceeds of his various crimes and the women in his life. Johnson had one real talent, though; he knew how to manipulate vulnerable women.

Johnson was known to harbor animosity towards women that would manifest when one crossed him in any sort of way. Violence was an option that Johnson routinely employed when things did not go his way. He would beat his girlfriends if they did not listen to him and he was known to have been abusive towards his wife at the time in 1979.

That was when Susan Schwarz and Gregory Johnson's paths fatefully crossed.

As Johnson put his wife through numerous rounds of physical and mental abuse, Susan Schwarz stepped in to help by bringing the abused woman to a shelter. According to acquaintances of both Johnson and Schwarz, Johnson resented what he considered to be Schwarz's tampering with his relationship. No way would a woman tell Gregory Johnson what to do.

When the investigators learned of this development, Johnson went to the top of their suspect list.

Although the revelations of Johnson's criminal behavior and the fact that he knew Susan Schwarz were helpful to investigators, it was not enough to make an arrest. The investigators needed an eye-witness and/or physical evidence that could place him at the scene of the crime.

Unfortunately, they had neither.

The Snohomish County investigators had a feeling that Johnson was their man, so they doggedly interviewed all of his friends and associates, but none would give him up. They also questioned Johnson on two different occasions, but he never admitted to the crime and in fact even implicated his brother at one point.

Susan Schwarz's murder drew considerable media attention in the Seattle area after it happened, but when no arrest was made, the coverage soon evaporated. As the weeks after the murder turned to months and then years, many thought that the crime would never be solved.

The members of the Snohomish County Sheriff's Department began to fear that Gregory Johnson had gotten away with murder.

It's All in the Cards

The solving of "cold" murder cases has attracted significant media attention in recent years. Many cold cases and the procedures used by investigators to solve them have been profiled on television documentary programs like *Forensic Files* and the *New Detectives*, but Susan Schwarz's case differed from most of those. In many of those cases, the police have no idea of who the killers are and the cases are usually solved with the assistance of advances in forensic science.

In the Susan Schwarz murder case, the investigators were quite confident they knew the identity of the killer and advances in forensic science would not help their case.

They needed to find a new witness using a new method.

In the early 2000s, like many major police departments around the United States, the Snohomish County Sherriff's Department created a Cold Case Team in order to solve their backlog of unsolved murders. Some of their unsolved cases were solved through advances in forensic science, but for the ones that could not be solved through science, investigators came up with the idea of putting the victims on playing cards and sending them to jails and prisons throughout Washington.

It did not take long for the cards to pay off.

When Patrick VanderWyst joined the Snohomish County Sherriff's Department Cold Case Team in 2010, he took the position with a sense of vigor. Not long after he began work with the Cold Case Team, he received a tip from an inmate in the Washington State Department of Corrections.

The inmate told VanderWyst that Johnson had once bragged to him about killing a woman who dared help his abused wife. He said that he forgot about it until he saw Susan's picture on the cold case victim's playing cards. The detective was skeptical about the story; inmates routinely approach law enforcement officers with stories in order to get their sentences reduced, receive more privileges while in prison, and sometimes just to get out of their cells. But after listening to the inmate's story, something told VanderWyst that this confession was legitimate. The inmate related details that only someone with intimate knowledge of the crime would know and the individual also seemed genuinely disturbed by the entire situation.

VanderWyst knew that this was an important break in the case, but one that they probably could not use in court. He needed more to get a conviction, or even an arrest for that matter. Upon interviewing the inmate in prison, VanderWyst learned that Johnson had a girlfriend at the time of the murder who the original investigators never interviewed because they did not know about her.

After doing some detective work, the Cold Case Team was finally able to locate Johnson's former girlfriend, who was a teenager at the time of Susan's murder. The investigators were hoping that the former girlfriend could possibly relate some more information about the crime—the location of the murder weapon, for instance—that could help them arrest Johnson.

They were shocked to learn so much more.

When VanderWyst sat down with Johnson's former girlfriend, he listened for hours as the woman told him a heartbreaking story of abuse and murder. Gregory's former girlfriend stated that on the day of the murder, he made her ride along with him to Susan Schwarz's home. She claimed that she did not know he was going to murder her, but once everything began, there was little she could do to stop it.

She watched Johnson bind and then shoot Schwarz three times, after which he turned to her and said: "It's that easy. This is what happens to people who fuck with my life."

In order to keep the one witness to the murder silent, Johnson threatened her both physically and legally. He told her that if she told anyone about the murder that he would find out before the police caught him and that he would kill her, or he would have one of his criminal associates do the deed. He added that he had the power to kill her family and that she would watch them die before she was murdered. Johnson also told her that since she was at the scene of the crime, then she would be implicated as an accessory and therefore face a lengthy prison sentence.

As the years after the murder elapsed, Johnson and his girlfriend, who remains anonymous, drifted apart. Johnson was in and out of prison numerous times and his former girlfriend tried to put her life back together. When detective VanderWyst contacted her, she knew she had to come clean.

Based on Johnson's ex-girlfriend's statement, Gregory Johnson was arrested and charged with the murder of Susan Schwarz. Knowing that his former girlfriend's testimony would have been damning and in order to avoid a possible death sentence, Johnson pled guilty to second degree murder in January 2012. He was sentenced to a minimum of twenty four years in prison, which essentially amounts to a life sentence for the fifty-eight-year old.

The Aftermath

Although Susan Schwarz's murder was solved through a combination of keen detective work and a novel tactic, and not due to advances in forensic technology, it has become a template for cold case investigators around the country. Other cold case squads have adopted the playing cards as a technique to help solve cold cases when there is a lack of forensic evidence.

The unique status of the case also led to its feature in an episode of the Investigation Discovery channel's program, *Motives and Murders: Cracking the Case*, in 2012.

Besides the professional and popular interest that the solving of the Susan Schwarz case garnered, it helped provide closure for her still living family members.

"When she died, I wrapped her memory in blankets and tried to forget it," said Susan's now elderly father, Henry Schwarz.

Fortunately for the Schwarz family, Patrick VanderWyst and the Snohomish County Sherriff's Department Cold Case Team did not forget the murder of Susan Schwarz.

The Cold Case Team is now working on their next card.

CHAPTER 2:
Victor Licata and "Reefer Madness"

Human use of the drug cannabis, in the form of the naturally growing weed marijuana, has been documented for several centuries. The fifth century BC Greek historian, Herodotus, wrote about how the Scythians would burn marijuana in sweat lodges to attain otherworldly visions. In the centuries since that time, marijuana remained on the fringes of most societies: it was there but rarely acknowledged by the authorities and therefore defacto legal.

In the United States, thanks to tireless propaganda efforts by the government and other organizations, attitudes toward marijuana began to change in the 1930s. A spate of anti-marijuana films, the most famous of which was *Reefer Madness*, were produced during the '30s that depicted the supposed pitfalls of marijuana use. The films portrayed marijuana use as leading to promiscuity, accidents, and even cold-blooded murder.

Although the propaganda films are viewed as humorous and over the top campy, they served their purpose effectively as the United States Congress passed the Marijuana Tax Act of 1937, which made the possession and use of marijuana illegal throughout the country.

But laws and attitudes often change.

Beginning in the 1960s, advocates for the legalization of marijuana began to organize into legitimate political lobby organizations. Pro-marijuana advocates faced an uphill battle, but by the 1990s they had managed to change many Americans' opinions about the illicit drug as referendums were passed in many states allowing marijuana for medical use. Today, three states—Colorado, Washington, and Oregon—have legalized marijuana for recreational use and several other states either allow for medical use or have decriminalized marijuana in small amounts.

The tide seems to have turned in marijuana's favor in the United States, with opponents taking a more logical stance against the drug. Those opposed to the liberalization of marijuana laws in the United States no longer argue that the drug makes one violent or sex crazed, but instead contend that marijuana is a gateway to harder drugs and that it leads to health problems.

Many Americans today wonder why marijuana was even criminalized in the first place. Sure, the propaganda films such as *Refer Madness* played a role, but one real-life crime probably contributed more to the ban on marijuana in the United States than any film—the 1933 murder of the Licata family in Tampa, Florida.

A Brutal Axe Murder

The legal status of marijuana was the last thing most Americans had on their minds in 1933. The country was in the midst of the Great Depression, the Dust Bowl had gripped the plains states, and Europe appeared to be ripping itself apart as numerous countries dropped democracy in favor of fascism and communism.

The vast majority of Americans never saw marijuana and most did not care who did the drug. People were more concerned about putting food on their families' tables.

The Depression took hold of Florida just as bad as any other state in the country, but fortunately for the Licata family, the patriarch, Michael, had built a successful, depression-proof business.

Michael Licata owned two barbershops in the Tampa Bay area, which proved to be especially resilient when the Depression hit; men always need haircuts, especially when they are looking for work. Michael Licata not only built a successful business, but was also a proud husband and father of an all-American family. Besides father Michael, the Licata family included: forty-four-year-old mother Rosalie, twenty-two-year-old daughter Prudence and three sons; twenty-year-old Victor, fourteen-year-old Phillip, and eight-year-old Jose.

Michael and Rosalie were active in their local Catholic Church and Italian-American organizations. They were also friendly with all of their neighbors. Since the entire Licata family lived in the same home, it was common to see different family members coming and going from the house throughout the day.

On October 17, 1933, the Licata house was eerily quiet.

When a day had passed and the neighbors had yet to see any members of the Licata family enter or leave the family home, they decided to call the police.

The police were shocked by what they found.

A Bloodbath Uncovered

When the Tampa police responded to concerned calls from the Licata's neighbors, they were not prepared for what they would find. The responding officers found the home unlocked and the lights off. They entered the home slowly and realized that for some reason their shoes were sticking to the floor. One of the officers turned on a light, which is when the house of horrors was revealed.

The bodies of Michael, Rosalie, Prudence, Phillip, and Jose were strewn about the house, hacked-up bloody messes.

The police quickly determined that the killer had used an axe on the Licata family in a most proficient manner.

Stepping over bodies and body parts, the police searched the house for any survivors.

In the bathroom, the police found Victor shivering and cowering, wearing clean clothes. After the police helped Victor up, they realized that he was bloody underneath the clothes so the officers removed his shirt to check for wounds but found none.

It appeared that Victor was the killer!

Victor was quickly brought to the police station for questioning, but the officers involved soon learned that he was no ordinary suspect. Victor readily admitted to the murders, but claimed they were done in self-defense. Wondering how someone could claim such horrific murders were done in self-defense, the detectives pressed Victor further for answers.

The detectives were blown away by Victor's bizarre story.

Victor claimed that all of the members of his family, including his youngest brother, had been conspiring against him for some time. He believed that they were planning to torture and ultimately kill him. Just before the murders they had finally carried out their nefarious plan against him by chopping off his arms and then replacing them with wooden arms and iron claws.

Victor was adamant that he had to kill them in order to keep from being further victimized.

After taking Victor's statement and looking into his background, the police and the courts knew that Victor was a mentally disturbed man who should go to a mental hospital. Insanity defenses were much more common at that time and were often successful. With that said, the institutions where they sent those deemed mentally unfit for trial were often worse than prison.

But many in the press and the government used the tragic murders for political purposes.

The Licata Killings, Yellow Journalism, and the Crusade against Marijuana

Although it is known now, and was at the time by most people involved with the case, the Licata killings was a case of improperly diagnosed mental illness, it did not let some turn the situation into an anti-marijuana crusade.

The local newspapers, without any corroborating evidence, claimed that Victor Licata was a regular marijuana user and that his heavy use of the drug ultimately led to his insanity and the murder of his family.

The truth is that there was no evidence that Viktor Licata was a regular marijuana user or that he had ever even tried the drug.

Also, no health care professionals were consulted for any of the articles.

Although mental health professionals were not consulted for any of the newspaper articles about the grisly murders, the opinions of Henry Anslinger, the first commissioner of the Federal Bureau of Narcotics, played a prominent role.

"An entire family was murdered by a youthful addict in Florida," wrote Anslinger. "When officers arrived at the home, they found the youth staggering about in a human slaughterhouse. With an axe he had killed his father, mother, two brothers and a sister. He seemed to be in a daze. He had no recollection of having committed the multiple crimes. The officers knew him ordinarily as a sane, rather quiet young man; now he was pitifully crazed. They sought the reason. They said that he had been in the habit of smoking something which youthful friends called 'muggles.' A childish name for marijuana."

With those statements, the perfect boogeyman for the anti-marijuana lobby was created. He was a delusional, axe-wielding young man who would kill even those closest to him due to the effects of marijuana.

But those closest to the case knew the reality was quite different.

Victor Licata's Mental Health

As the newspapers and government officials were using the Licata murder case as an example of the dangers of marijuana consumption, the prosecutors and judge realized that mental illness, not marijuana, was the true catalyst for the horrific murders. Victor Licata had a long documented battle with mental illness. Part of the reason he still lived with his parents was because he had a difficult time surviving in the outside world. His condition was so bad that he could not hold down a regular job and had a difficult time being around anyone outside of his immediate family. Today, some mental health professionals who have studied the Licata case believe that he suffered from early on-set dementia.

After all of the facts came to light, just two weeks after the murders, Victor Licata was declared mentally unfit to stand trial and was committed to the Florida State Hospital for the insane. Licata lingered in the hospital for nearly twenty years until he hanged himself in 1950, which marked the tragic end to a very strange and tragic case.

In the decades since the Licata murders, attitudes toward mental health and marijuana have changed considerably in the United States, almost somewhat ironically when one considers this case. Today, in some states, people with a medical permit are allowed to consume marijuana legally in order to alleviate the same mental problems for which Victor Licata suffered.

Perhaps if Victor Licata would have been allowed to consume marijuana this horrible crime would have never happened.

CHAPTER 3:
The Scott Peterson Murder Trial

In the modern world we live in, marriage is often a difficult prospect. Statistics show that over forty percent of first marriages and up to sixty percent of second marriages end in divorce. There are numerous reasons for couples to divorce. Infidelity is one of the more common reasons for a marriage to end, but other reasons include financial problems, abuse, and the couple simply "growing apart."

Divorces can be extremely expensive and emotionally draining for both sides, especially if children are involved. Alimony payments can make an amicable divorce contentious and custody and visitation rights concerning children are often a source of problems for many years after the final divorce papers are signed. For most people trapped in a difficult, loveless marriage, though, divorce is the only option.

But some turn to murder!

Statistically speaking, spousal murders usually comprise about one third of all murders in the United States—which includes both male partners killing female and vice versa, although the overwhelming majority of the spousal murder cases are committed by the male against the female—making them a somewhat rare occurrence. Unlike depictions on popular crime shows like *Law and Order: Special Victims Unit*, most spousal murders are unplanned and instead take place in the heat of the moment. A spouse may snap and kill his/her partner when he/she is confronted with a revelation concerning infidelity or finances.

But sometimes spousal murders are well planned.

In the rare case where a spousal murder is planned, the case usually makes for excellent tabloid television, and, once the case is decided, is often used for the basis of a fictionalized television or movie account.

The 2002 murder of Laci Peterson and the subsequent trial of her husband Scott was a case of pre-mediated spousal murder, complete with several twists and turns that provided ample fodder for the tabloids and non-stop entertainment for true crime junkies.

Two Lives Intersect

The way in which Scott Peterson and Laci Rocha met and became a couple was nothing out of the ordinary. Scott was born in 1972 to an upper-middle-class family in San Diego, California. Scott's early life was uninspiring for the most part. He was not known to be a trouble-maker in school and brought home average to good report cards on a regular basis. He enjoyed taking camping trips with his family, which is where he first developed a love for nature that he eventually turned into a career.

Two of the traits observed in Scott from an early age were his confidence and charisma. Scott was known to take over conversations during parties and other social gatherings. He was polite and always knew the right words to say, but to some who knew him better he sometimes seemed to be a wolf in sheep's clothing.

And his confidence seemed to border on arrogance to others.

When Scott graduated from high school, he went on to college at the California Polytechnic University in San Louis Obispo, California. Located approximately half way between San Francisco and Los Angeles, in the mountains of California's central coast, San Louis Obispo is home to nearly 50,000 residents, not including the university. Most people may not immediately think of California as an agricultural state, but its Central Valley produces many of the fresh fruits and vegetables found daily in supermarkets across the United States. California Polytechnic University was established to train young Californians to work and manage the numerous farms and ranches throughout the state.

Since childhood, Scott dreamed of both making a lot of money and working in the agricultural sector so when he went to school at California Polytechnic, he pursued a bachelor's of science degree in agricultural business, which he earned in 1997.

While working on his degree, the affable and attractive Peterson earned some spending money by working as a waiter at a San

Louis Obispo restaurant, which is where he met his future wife, Laci Rocha, in 1996. Laci was immediately attracted to Peterson's charm and looks. He told her that he wanted to start a family someday, which is exactly what the young woman wanted to hear.

To those that knew them, they seemed like the perfect couple.

Laci Rocha was born in 1975 to a middle class family in the Central Valley city of Modesto, California. Like Scott, Laci came from a small family, with one older brother and a younger half-sister from her father's second marriage.

In high school, Laci received good grades and was a popular student and a cheerleader. Also like Scott, Laci had a keen interest in nature and wanted to make a career out of that interest, so she packed up her bags and went to California Polytechnic University when she graduated from high school.

The attractive young brunette decided to study ornamental horticulture in college with the hope of one day owning her own floral business. When she met Scott Peterson in 1996, the two quickly became infatuated with each other, which resulted in a whirlwind courtship and marriage in August 1997, just before Laci graduated.

After Scott and Laci married, they moved to her hometown of Modesto to be close to her family and it was also a prime location for Scott's work.

The Disappearance of Laci Peterson

The first few years of Scott and Laci's marriage were for the most part uneventful. Some husbands would have a difficult time living so close to their in-laws, but Scott Peterson maintained relatively good relations with Laci's family. There was no evidence that he ever abused Laci, physically or emotionally.

With that said, the newlywed couple did have one problem— conceiving a child.

After the first couple of years of marriage, Laci began to yearn for a child. Reportedly, Laci's desire for a child was not shared with Scott. As the marriage entered its fifth year, there were signs that not only did Scott not want a child, but that he did not want to be married.

The situation changed when Laci revealed to Scott and their families that she was pregnant in early 2002.

During Laci's pregnancy, Scott played the role of dutiful husband and future father. He went with Laci to pre-natal classes and doctor visits. He even helped pick out a name for their future son—Connor. But, like many other aspects of Scott's life, it was just a façade. Underneath the cool exterior was a man who desperately wanted out of his marriage.

Scott found himself trapped in a situation from which it would be difficult to extricate himself. A divorce would be costly in terms of the lawyer and the fact that Laci would be entitled to half of all their property and assets according to California law, which is to say nothing about eighteen years of child support payments.

Scott Peterson would have to find another way to get out of his marriage.

December 23 was the last day that anyone other than Scott saw Laci alive. According to her friends and family, Laci spent most of the day making preparations for Christmas while Scott worked. Later that evening, Laci's sister Amy Rocha stopped by the Peterson home to visit her sister and give Scott a haircut. Laci then spoke with her mother on the phone for a while before turning in for the night.

Christmas Eve was a cool, quiet day in Modesto, as most of the Petersons' neighbors were either making their final Christmas preparations or had already left town to visit friends and family.

An eerie calm descended on the Petersons' neighborhood.

The first signs that something was amiss at the Peterson household came when one of their neighbors, Karen Servas, found the family's golden retriever wandering aimlessly through the neighborhood. The neighbor thought the situation was strange because the Petersons were generally responsible pet owners and never let their dog out without a leash. The neighbor walked the dog back to the Peterson home and rang the doorbell, but there was no answer. The confused neighbor became even more puzzled when she noticed that Laci's car was in the driveway. She looked in the front window and noticed that a purse was on the counter.

Thinking that Laci was possibly in the bathroom and the dog had simply got loose when she was not looking, Servas tied the dog up in the yard and went about her day.

Scott returned home in the early evening and called Sharon Rocha around 5:20 to ask if Laci was at her house. When she replied that she had not seen nor heard from her daughter all day, Scott replied, "Laci's missing."

The Rocha family immediately barraged Scott with a host of questions, namely why he was not at home with his wife on Christmas Eve. Scott was vague with the Rocha family concerning the last time he saw Laci and where he was all day. Eventually, he told them that he had been fishing all day in the San Francisco Bay and that the last time he saw Laci was very early in the morning.

Although the story sounded a bit fishy to the Rocha family, they accepted their son-in-law's story at face value.

The Rochas called the Modesto Police Department at six pm to report Laci missing and almost immediately a manhunt was underway for the missing expectant mother. Since Laci was pregnant, the police bypassed the normal twenty-four hour waiting period for missing adults.

Scores of Laci's friends and family and hundreds of volunteers showed up the next day to search for her, but as the Holidays came and went there was still no sign of Laci. A website was set up and rewards were offered for any information that would lead to the discovery of Laci, but no credible tips came.

Sure, there were some outlandish claims that Laci was abducted by either a satanic cult or a biker gang, but the local police never considered those very reliable. That fact is that when a spouse goes missing, as in the case of Laci Peterson, the police usually focus their attention close to home.

As the Petersons and Rochas searched for Laci, the police began to focus more and more on Scott.

Suspicious Scott

For his part, Scott Peterson initially played the role of distraught husband quite well. He gave a statement to the police and was cooperative with follow up interviews. Scott was also at the command center to locate Laci every day, answering phone calls and helping with other logistics.

But the attention was intense and eventually the façade that Scott had built up began to crack.

The case seemed tailor made for the national media: an attractive, all-American woman mysteriously disappears on Christmas Eve and her equally attractive, all-American husband is paralyzed with grief. Millions of Americans who followed the case prayed that Laci would return home alive.

But some in the media were skeptical of the entire situation.

The often caustic and always polarizing former prosecutor and talk show host, Nancy Grace, took a personal interest in the disappearance of Laci Peterson and did not hide the fact that she thought Scott was somehow involved. Repeatedly, on her eponymously named show on the Headline News Network, Grace exhorted Scott to be more forthcoming. Grace challenged Scott to "be a man" and tell the police everything.

Apparently, the focus that Grace and other members of the media gave to the case made Scott crack. In one particular press conference, reporters kept asking Scott to clarify his alibi and if the police thought that he was a suspect. Unable to answer the questions, Peterson stormed out of the press conference in a fit of anger.

After the conference, Scott Peterson quit giving interviews to the press and the police.

But the Modesto Police were working their own angle to the case.

While Scott Peterson was playing the role of concerned spouse, investigators with the Modesto Police Department began to look more closely at Peterson's background. The investigators looked hard to uncover any criminal or drug activity that may have led Scott to kill his wife. They also checked his financial records, but Scott turned up clean in all of those regards.

It turns out that Scott Peterson thought of himself as a ladies' man who was not willing to let a little thing like marriage stop his dalliances. The police were shocked to learn that not only was he involved with another woman when Laci disappeared, but that he continued to see the woman as if nothing happened to his wife.

The woman was twenty-eight-year-old Fresno, California massage therapist Amber Frey, who unknowingly began to date Peterson just before Laci disappeared. The police learned that Frey, who is a tall, attractive blonde, and Peterson met via a business associate of Scott's. In October of 2002, Scott was at a convention representing his company, Tradecrop, when he ran into a female acquaintance. The two had a few drinks in the hotel's lounge when Scott told her that he was single and a "horny bastard." Finding Peterson cute and believable, Scott's friend then introduced him to Frey in November and the two began dating soon thereafter.

In what was essentially a self-fulfilling prophecy that telegraphed his homicidal plan, Peterson told Fry in a phone conversation on December 9, 2002, just two weeks before Laci went missing, that his wife was dead and it would be the first Christmas without her!

For some reason, even with the immense media coverage, Peterson thought that Frey would never learn about his other life and so he continued to pursue her.

But while Peterson was whispering sweet nothings into Frey's ears on the phone, investigators with the Modesto Police were also speaking with her.

In what was perhaps the best example of Peterson's confidence turning into arrogance, he continued to pursue Frey even as he gave press conferences. Frey eventually saw the news reports of her boyfriend and was shocked to learn that not only was he married, but even more worrisome, he pregnant wife was missing.

Confused and hurt, Frey discussed the situation with some family members and close friends and decided that she needed to go to the police and tell them what she knew.

The Modesto Police laid out the whole situation for Frey, who quickly retained the services of well-known feminist attorney, Gloria Allred. Despite retaining a high-powered attorney, Frey was angry and confused about the situation, so she agreed to help the police by allowing them to record their conversations. Although Peterson never admitted to killing Laci in any of his conversations with Frey, the phone calls made him look bad and were used by police and prosecutors as evidence for a motive to kill his wife.

The case against Scott Peterson looked bad, but without a body it would be hard to charge him with any crime.

The Discovery of Laci's Body

For the first few months of 2003, the Modesto Police and Scott Peterson played a sort of cat and mouse game. Peterson did whatever he could to avoid the police and reporters, while the police continued to collect circumstantial evidence against him.

When his affair with Frey was revealed in the press, Scott lost most of his supporters and public opinion turned sharply against him. The Rocha family knew in their hearts that Scott must have done something to Laci, yet he walked the streets free.

Until Laci's body was discovered.

On the morning of April 13, 2003, a couple walking along the beach of the San Francisco Bay near Berkley made a gruesome discovery. At first they did not know what they had found lying on the shore, but after they examined the pile of debris more closely they were shocked to learn that it was the remains of a human.

It was later determined that the remains were that of a fetus, which was that of Laci and Scott's unborn son, later officially named Connor by the Rocha family. Nylon cords were around the body and it had a significant gash. It was not immediately known if the gash was a post-mortem injury or not.

The police believed that they had discovered Laci's unborn child, but they could not be sure until a DNA test was done on the corpse. The next day, their thoughts were confirmed when the decomposed body of a recently pregnant female washed ashore near the same place as the fetus. DNA testing revealed that the adult body was that of Laci Peterson and the fetus was that of unborn Connor. The fact that the fetus was separate from the mother raised speculation and conspiracy theories that were floated in the press and later by Scott Peterson's defense attorney. The investigators believe that Laci's body was decapitated, either before she was dumped into the bay or later, as the result of being hit by a boat, with the fetus disconnecting from her body later.

Once it was confirmed that the bodies were that of Laci and her son, a warrant was issued for the arrest of Scott Peterson.

The Arrest and Trial of Scott Peterson

When the warrant for Scott Peterson's arrest was issued, the police wasted no time and promptly went to his home to make an arrest.

Scott was nowhere to be found.

Unable to locate Peterson in Modesto, investigators received a tip that he was spending time with his family in southern California. Investigators moved quickly to arrest Peterson, who they captured playing golf with family members in the San Diego suburb of La Jolla, California. Peterson was arrested without incident, but the arresting officers were surprised to find the items in his possession.

In Peterson's car, the police found his brother's driver's license and they noticed that he had dyed his hair and goatee bleach blond. It appeared to the police that Peterson may have been planning to abscond rather than face charges and a further search of his car revealed even more disturbing details.

Inside the car were some camping equipment, four cell phones, and a rope and a shovel. It appears that Peterson was planning to live off the grid for a while, but he may have planned to exact some revenge before he left. There was also a MapQuest map to Amber Frey's work, which many believe indicates Peterson was planning to kill his lover turned police informant before he left town.

Peterson was brought back to Modesto where he was placed in the Stanislaus County Jail to await trial.

There would be no bail for Scott Peterson!

Although Peterson was not able to bail out of jail while he awaited trial, his family was able to raise enough money to hire high-profile defense attorney, Mark Geragos for him. Geragos made his mark in the legal profession by defending Bill Clinton associate Susan McDougal during the 1990s and Winona Ryder in 2002, but the Scott Peterson trial would be one of his toughest tasks.

Geragos repeatedly tried to use the media to his client's advantage by giving press conferences and appearing on news programs where he argued that Peterson was being tried solely for his character, or lack thereof. He argued that his client was a cad, but no killer and that there was very little evidence to suggest he was.

After about a year of pre-trial hearings, the trial finally got underway in early 2004.

Geragos was correct; there was very little physical evidence linking his client to Laci's and Connor's murders, but he consistently left out that there was a mountain of circumstantial evidence pointing toward Peterson's guilt.

The prosecution took months to present its case to the jury. They called numerous witnesses and presented copious amounts of evidence, but missing was a "smoking gun" in the form of eye-witnesses that saw Peterson commit the murder. There was also a lack of forensic evidence that could tie Peterson to the murders. No murder weapon was found and Peterson had no physical marks on his body that would indicate a struggle. None of Laci's blood was in the Peterson family home, where prosecutors believe the murder took place, and the advanced stage of decomposition of Laci's body meant that the killer's DNA could not be taken from her. This was a definite problem for the prosecution. Because we are inundated with a plethora of forensic science based crime shows, both fictional and documentary, people today tend to be a bit more skeptical of crime cases that lack physical evidence.

But there is no law that physical evidence is needed to convict a person, only that a jury has to be convinced of the defendant's guilt beyond a reasonable doubt.

When the prosecution began presenting its case against Peterson, it quickly became clear to all in the courtroom and the millions across the United States who were following the trial on Court TV that the circumstantial evidence against him was damning. Some of the most incriminating evidence presented against Peterson included the fact that he sold Laci's car not long after she disappeared, but before her body was discovered. There was concrete discovered in Peterson's storage unit that was consistent with blocks used to weigh Laci down in the San Francisco Bay. Then there were the pornography channels Scott ordered for their home not long after Laci went missing. And of course there was Amber Frey's testimony and the evidence of other extra-marital dalliances by Scott Peterson.

But perhaps the most incriminating bit of circumstantial evidence came from Scott Peterson's own mouth.

Peterson's alibi was that he spent most of Christmas Eve fishing in the San Francisco Bay. Although the Bay is a very large body of water, Peterson was able to accurately tell investigators the part of the Bay where he spent most of the day. Investigators turned Peterson's statement over to Rick Cheng, a hydrologist with the United States Geological Survey, who then testified that the location where Laci's and Connor's bodies washed ashore would be consistent with Scott dumping them from the boat where he claimed he was fishing.

In fact, the only physical evidence that the prosecution presented that possibly tied Scott to his wife's murder was a pliers discovered in his storage unit that had a single hair on it that was consistent with Laci's. But the prosecution believed that the one piece of physical evidence, combined with the mountain of circumstantial evidence, was enough to convict Peterson.

When the prosecution rested it was confident that it presented a logical, open and shut case against Peterson. They argued that he was tired of his marriage and instead of going through a costly divorce and years of child support payments, he strangled his wife in their home, loaded her into the boat, and then disposed of the corpse in the San Francisco Bay.

Courtroom observers and professional legal pundits were impressed with the prosecution's case, but eagerly waiting what high-profile attorney Mark Geragos would do for his client.

Once the defense began its case, those observers were sorely disappointed.

Geragos' defense of Scott Peterson can best be described as vague and uneven. The defense floated numerous alternate theories concerning how Laci may have been murdered, including at the hands of a satanic cult and/or meth-crazed ex-convicts. The theories were of course meant to sow the seeds of doubt in the minds of the jury, but they only seemed to confuse them.

One of the star defense witnesses was supposed to be Dr. Charles March, who testified that Connor died about a week after what prosecutors claimed. Under cross examination, though, March recanted some of what he said and looked confused and bewildered on the stand. As one observer noted: "By the end of his testimony Thursday, legal analysts and jurors closed their notebooks, rolled their eyes, and snickered when they thought no one was looking."

And although Peterson never took the stand in his own defense, his body language as he sat next to his lawyer did not help. Scott was often seen gazing around the courtroom, smiling at inappropriate times, and generally acting as if the whole case was one big bother to him.

After nearly nine months of trial, Scott Peterson was convicted of two counts of first degree murder on November 12, 2004.

Although California is a liberal state politically speaking, the death penalty is an option in capital murder trials. The jury voted for the death penalty on December 13, and on March 16, 2005, Judge Alfred A. Delucci concurred and sentenced Scott Peterson to death.

Delucci noted that Peterson was particularly "cruel, uncaring, heartless, and callous" and was more than deserving of the sentence.

Scott Peterson now sits on death row in the historic San Quentin prison, which ironically overlooks the San Francisco Bay where he dumped his wife's and unborn son's bodies.

The Aftermath

For a number of reasons, the Scott Peterson murder case is one that continues to come back up in the headlines from time to time. More than ten years later, the case continues to be featured in true crime documentaries and fictionalized depictions. The murders of Laci and Connor even led to new federal laws being enacted.

On April 1, 2004, President George W. Bush signed into law the Unborn Victims of Violence Act, often referred to as "Laci's and Connor's Law", which recognizes unborn children as victims of violent crime. The Rocha family was integral in lobbying for the law and continue to work on behalf of victims' rights.

The conviction was also not the last time the public has heard from

Scott Peterson.

Using his Constitutional rights, Peterson has appealed both his conviction and sentence, but to no avail so far. Occasionally, reports of Peterson's life behind bars surface. One report from the *National Enquirer* stated that Peterson ran afoul of the notorious serial killer the "Night Stalker" Richard Ramirez over a drug debt. The article stated that Peterson was helped out of the situation by another inmate in return for sexual favors. It is difficult to ascertain the validity of the article, but death row in California is one of the only such units in the United States where the inmates in the cell block are allowed free time on the yard and in the block, so it is perfectly reasonable.

Since California's death row inmates are allowed numerous appeals, they are rarely executed. On November 8, 2016, the voters of California will decide in a referendum if the death penalty will be abolished in the state, or if the tax-payers will fund more public defenders to handle death penalty appeals, which will ultimately increase the number of executions carried out.

Whatever Californians decide, there is a good probability that we will hear from Scott Peterson again, whether we like it or not!

CHAPTER 4:
The Trial of Football Superstar Rae Carruth

Sports stars have long played key role in American culture. The names of athletes such as Babe Ruth, Hank Aaron, and Joe Namath have been immortalized in the annals of American sports history and their images are easily recognizable to sports fans of all ages. American professional athletes represent a truly privileged class; their sometimes astronomical salaries and fame make them sources of envy and adulation for millions of people.

The majority of most American professional athletes handle the fame and money quite well and many even use their wealth and visibility to help less fortunate people.

But then there are the athletes who take their sense of entitlement too far.

In recent years, there seems to have been a rash of major crimes committed by American professional athletes. Mike Tyson's 1992 rape conviction, former NBA player Jayson Williams' 2010 assault conviction, and former NFL player Darren Sharper's recent spate of cross-country rape convictions are just three of the most recent high-profile cases of professional athletes falling from grace. There have also been a number of recent sexual assaults committed by athletes at major American universities, most notably Baylor, which have garnered media attention and both criminal and civil legal proceedings.

With that said, murders committed by professional American athletes are still very rare and premeditated murder plots are almost unheard of.

In 1999, during the middle of the National Football League's regular season, a well-planned, but not so well executed, murder took place that involved one of the league's brightest young stars.

Against the Odds

Rae Carruth, like many of the players in the NFL, came from humble origins. He was born Rae Lamar Wiggins in 1974 to a poor family in Sacramento, California. Rae grew up in a hardscrabble black neighborhood where crime and conflict were a part of daily life. Some of his friends and neighbors lost their lives to violence on the streets of Sacramento during the 1980s and were it not for Rae's natural abilities, he may also have succumbed to the same fate.

At an early age Rae was noted by his teachers and coaches for his athletic abilities, particularly his speed and ability to leap higher than most other kids his age. Rae excelled in track and football in high school, which earned him several visits from college recruiters from around the country.

Rae's athletic abilities gave him a ticket out of poverty.

After mulling over the slate of division one scholarship offers that he had received, Rae decided to take his talents to play football at the University of Colorado in Boulder, Colorado. Rae made an immediate impact on the field in the position of wide receiver, being voted All-American in 1996 and earning the nickname "Da Troof."

But off the field, things were a little more complicated.

While playing for Colorado, Rae had a child with his girlfriend Michelle Wright, which brought to the surface Carruth's lack of maturity that would get him into trouble later. Instead of happiness, Carruth was angry with the situation, refused to pay child support, and cut off communication with Wright for the remainder of his time at Boulder.

Although Carruth eventually began making child support payments, he had nothing to do with his child. He had plans to play in the NFL and his child would only slow him down.

Rae Carruth could not be bothered with such petty things. He had bigger things in store for his life!

Rae Carruth Makes the Bigtime

The chance of making the roster on a major professional sports team is infinitesimal at best. Despite the gift of genetics, hard work, and some luck, even the best college athletes never fulfill their dreams of playing in a major sports league.

You have a better chance of winning a lottery!

But in the spring of 1997, Rae Carruth hit the lottery when he was the twenty seventh pick of the first round in the NFL draft. Rae was drafted by what was then the fairly new franchise of the Carolina Panthers and given a four year contract worth over four million dollars.

Rae Carruth was clearly on his way up, apparently leaving the crime and violence of the mean streets of Sacramento behind him.

Carruth's rookie season was a blazing success. He started in fourteen of the Panthers' sixteen games, catching forty-four passes for 545 yards and four touchdowns, which was good for a tie among rookie wide receivers in the league. For his success on the field, Carruth was rewarded by being made a member of the league's all-rookie team for the 1997 season.

After the season, everyone in the Panthers' organization, as well as both local and national sports commentators, expected Carruth to play an even bigger role in the team's future. But unknown to them, Rae was slowly sliding into the dark side.

During the off-season, Carruth became a regular at a number of Charlotte night spots where he was often seen in the company of several women and some men with nefarious pasts. Carruth amassed an entourage of ex-cons, street thugs, and other assorted gold diggers. The situation only got worse when the 1998 NFL season began.

Carruth completed the 1998 training camp in good condition and was expected to play an even bigger role with the Panthers during that season. Unfortunately for Carruth, he broke his foot during the first game of the 1998 season and did not take the field again that year. He also played very little in the 1999 season. Placed on the injured reserve list for the 1998 season, Carruth had a lot of time on his hands.

Carruth did not spend his time constructively.

The Hit on Cherica Adams

Finding himself on the injured reserve list, Carruth was able to further indulge in the vices he picked up during his rookie season. Carruth spent even more time in the clubs, womanizing and hanging out with some of Charlotte's most notorious thugs, such as Van Brett Watkins Senior. Watkins, who is the size of an NFL linebacker, was working security at various clubs in the area, which is how he and Carruth met. Besides being a bouncer, Watkins had several connections to the criminal underworld and a lengthy rap sheet.

Most people would wonder why a professional athlete with a bright future would associate with criminals, especially ones that he did not know from his childhood. The situation is clearly another example of Carruth's immaturity and lack of confidence. Instead of surrounding himself with other successful people, Carruth found it easier to associate with losers he could order around.

Rae Carruth saw himself as a big fish in a small pond.

While Carruth was hanging out with Watkins at Charlotte area clubs, a young woman named Cherica Adams was one of the many females who he began dating. Adams, who was about one year younger than Rae, was looking for a stable relationship and thought she had found it with the rookie sensation.

The details concerning how the two met are a bit cloudy and there are conflicting stories. One story is that Rae met Cherica while she was a dancer at a strip club, while another report states that the two were introduced by a teammate of Rae's. At the time of her death, Cherica was working as a real-estate agent in order to build a better life for herself and the child she was going to have with Rae.

According to Rae's associates, he wanted nothing to do with the pregnancy.

In a repeat of his college days, Rae was upset when he learned that not only was Cherica pregnant, but that she planned to have the baby. Carruth told friends that the situation would ruin his finances and that it would hurt his chances with another woman he was romancing. He begged her to get an abortion, but Cherica would not hear of it.

Cherica Adams was having Rae Carruth's baby.

As Adams' pregnancy progressed, the only contact Carruth had with her was his repeated requests for her to get an abortion.

When Carruth finally got it through his head that she was going to have the baby, he decided to change his tactics.

Rae Carruth formulated a plot to end the pregnancy of Cherica Adams by taking her life!

Once the details of the murder plot were revealed, it became evident that it was a situation of the blind leading the blind. Although Carruth's co-conspirators had criminal experience, none were very bright and Rae himself was always known for his physical abilities, not his brains.

The initial plan called for Carruth's co-conspirators—Watkins and another man named Michael Kennedy—to ruthlessly gun down Adams outside of a movie theater while Rae was with her. The dimwitted trio believed that the police would determine the hit to be a robbery gone wrong and that no suspicion would be cast Carruth's way.

The first part of the plan went through without a hitch. Carruth was able to entice Adams to go to a movie with him, but his dimwitted cohorts called it off at the last minute. They were spooked by all the potential eyewitnesses in the parking lot so they packed up and went home.

Carruth probably should have rethought the entire scheme when the initial plan fell through, but being the entitled professional athlete that he was, he rescheduled the hit for another time and place.

Carruth and his witless cohorts were finally able to launch their diabolical scheme on the night of November 16, 1999, just after midnight. Carruth was in one car while Kennedy drove the other car with Watkins in the passenger seat as the gunman. When they caught up to Adams in a residential neighborhood of Charlotte, Rae blocked her BMW from the front while Kennedy pulled up alongside her and Watkins shot four times into her car.

The three then raced away from the crime scene.

The bumbling crooks made one vital mistake: Cherica Adams was severely wounded but not dead. She was able to make a call to 911 where she identified Carruth as the driver who blocked her car, allowing her to be shot. Adams was rushed to a Charlotte trauma center where she lapsed into a coma. Since Adams was eight months pregnant, doctors delivered her baby via Caesarian section, but unfortunately, because he was deprived of oxygen after the shooting, the boy was born with brain damage.

Carruth was quickly arrested by the Charlotte Police and charged with attempted murder, but allowed to post a three million dollar bond with the condition that if either Cherica Adams or her son, named Chancellor, died, then he would have to turn himself in on murder charges.

Cherica Adams lost her fight and died on December 14, 1999.

Running for His Life

Up until December 1999, Rae Carruth had spent most of his life running for a living. He gained great fame and money running up and down football fields for the Carolina Panthers, but after Adams died he decided to run for his life.

With the potential of facing a life sentence, or even the death penalty in the state of North Carolina, Carruth decided to abscond from his bond and hit the road.

But like the murder plot that got him arrested, Carruth's plan to evade justice showed a lack of foresight and intelligence.

Only one day after Adams died, Carruth was captured hiding in the trunk of a car in a hotel parking lot in western Tennessee. After the police searched the contents of his car, it became clear that Carruth did not consider the situation he was in very carefully. There were several bottles of urine in the car, which he used so that he did not have to pull over, and $3,900 in cash.

If the situation did not involve the death of a person and the crippling of another, it would be almost laughable. How long did someone with Carruth's expensive tastes think he would last on that amount of money?

Although this question was interesting, Carruth would face even bigger and more important ones when he was brought back to Charlotte and tried for Adams' murder.

The Trial

Since Carruth already absconded on his bond once, he was remanded to the Mecklenburg County Jail without bail. The trial was given intense coverage by both the local and national media and was shown daily on Court TV. The prosecution's case against Carruth rested on eyewitness testimony—the 911 phone call by Cherica Adams and the statements of his co-conspirator, Van Brett Watkins Senior.

Watkins' testimony in particular proved to be both damning for Carruth and a somewhat entertaining spectacle. The imposing Watkins, who pled guilty to second degree murder in exchange for a forty year sentence, repeatedly stared Carruth down from the witness stand and sometimes wandered from his testimony to directly address the jury.

For his part, Watkins attempted to mitigate his role in the murder.

"He hired me as a hit man," Watkins testified. "He hired me to kill Cherica Adams and the baby. . . I couldn't bring myself to kill the baby. I shot at the top [of the car], not through the door."

Later, though, Watkins admitted that he did shoot into the car with fatal consequences.

"I fired one shot, then four more shots—bam, bam, bam, bam," testified an animated Watkins. "She was screaming. She was drowning in her own blood. You could hear a gurgling sound."

Despite having a mountain of evidence stacked against their client,

Carruth's lawyers put up a spirited defense. They argued that Cherica Adams was simply at the wrong place at the wrong time. The true target was Carruth, who Watkins and Kennedy intended to kill as part of a large-scale marijuana trafficking scheme gone wrong.

The strategy was partially successful because when the jury came back with its verdict in early January 2001, Carruth was convicted of conspiracy to commit murder, but acquitted of the much more serious charge of first degree murder.

The hit man's driver, Michael Kennedy, was given an eleven year sentence for second degree murder.

Carruth was given an eighteen to twenty four year sentence in the North Carolina Department of Corrections. Currently, he is being housed in a low security facility and is scheduled for release in late 2018.

CHAPTER 5:
The Strange and Fascinating Life of Jack Kevorkian

Since the beginning of human civilization, mankind has pondered the nuances of life and death. The ancient Egyptians believed that death was only temporary and if a deceased person's body was preserved properly and buried with the correct implements, then one would live forever in the "Field of Reeds." Later, the Greek and Roman philosophers contemplated the nature of life and whether anything awaits us after death.

Central to some of these philosophers' ideas on life and death was the morality of the ability of an individual to end his or her life. The Stoics, who were popular with the Romans, believed that if an individual faced dishonor and there was nothing left to live for, then suicide was a perfectly acceptable option. Other ancient philosophers also took this position. Most famously, Socrates is said to have drunk a fatal dose of hemlock when facing trial in fifth century BC Athens.

In more modern times, no doubt due to the strong influence of Christianity in the West, suicide has taken on a negative image.

Some see suicide as morally reprehensible and a mortal sin, while others see it as a sign of mental illness.

Although it is true that many who commit suicide suffer from mental health issues, there are a percentage of people who decide to end their lives due to persistent physical pain in a truly Stoic fashion.

The idea of a right to die, usually because of persistent pain caused by terminal illness, has become a political issue in the United States over the last thirty years. Oregon, Washington, and Vermont have passed laws protecting an individual's "right to die," while it is a de facto right in Montana and laws are pending in California and New Mexico.

Many experts on the subject credit the increase in state laws that protect the right to die to one man—Jack Kevorkian, the "Doctor of Death."

A Student of Death

Jack Kevorkian was born in 1928 in the Detroit suburb of Pontiac, Michigan, to Armenian immigrant parents. Kevorkian's family life was stable, as his father was a successful contractor who was able to consistently work even through the Great Depression. Despite the stable family life, young Jack was familiarized with death at an early age.

Jack's mother immigrated to the United States from Turkey, where she witnessed first-hand the horrors of the genocide that the

Turkish government inflicted on the Armenian minority in that country. Although the horrors of the Armenian genocide were not discussed extensively in the Kevorkian household, young Jack heard enough about the situation to learn at an early age that humans were capable of inflicting immense pain and misery on other humans. On the other hand, Kevorkian learned through reading that humans were capable of alleviating the suffering of others, through medicine and euthanasia.

Kevorkian excelled in most subjects in primary and high school, but he was considered a bit of a rebel because he often questioned his teachers and the course material, which was considered taboo in 1930s America. Despite earning a reputation as a contrarian at an early point in his life, Kevorkian always respected others' rights. He never got into legal troubles and stayed out of physical altercations with other boys.

Young Jack Kevorkian was polite, amiable, and helpful, but to those who knew him, he clearly lived in a world of his own. While most boys his age were focused on sports, girls, and other socializing in general, Kevorkian was more interested in books and ideas. He spent most of his spare time reading and could be found in the library after school when most other kids his age were at the soda fountain.

Kevorkian's studious nature in high school paid off with scholarships for college and later medical school at the University of Michigan. His time in medical school was for the most part uneventful; he graduated with high marks in 1952 and then went to serve in the army as a medical officer in 1953.

The future Doctor of Death's hitch with the army brought him to Korea where he received his first intimate experiences with death. The year 1953 was the height of the Korean War and causalities began to pile up as the Americans fought hard to keep the Chinese and North Koreans from overwhelming South Korea.

Kevorkian became particularly interested witnessing soldiers at the precise moment of death. He paid special attention to the dying soldiers' eyes in order to see if something special took place.

"Really, my number one reason was because it was interesting," said Kevorkian on gazing into dying soldiers' eyes. "And my second reason was because it was a taboo subject."

It was there behind the front lines during the Korean War that Jack Kevorkian realized that he could combine his fascination with death and his rebellious attitude to make a career for himself and hopefully help the world. Kevorkian knew that it would be a long, uphill struggle for his ideas to gain acceptance within the academic and medical professions, but luckily for Kevorkian, he lived in his own world where the opinions of those opposed to him mattered little.

Kevorkian is best known today for being a practicing doctor, but his early medical career was primarily in the area of medical and academic research. He carefully crafted his observations from Korea in polished academic reports and papers that he later presented at medical conferences and then published in peer reviewed journals.

There was one problem with his research—once the war had ended, subjects were few and far between.

The young researcher came up with a solution that he presented at a 1958 medical conference: the use of death row inmates for experiments concerning death. Kevorkian termed his proposal "terminal human experimentation," which, as the title indicates, would have involved deadly experiments on death row inmates. As macabre as the proposal sounded at the time and still does today, Kevorkian was adamant that only inmates who volunteered for the experiments would be used. A doctor should never end a person's life without his or her consent he argued, but at the same time it was a person's right to end his or her life.

The majority of the medical community was astounded that one of their own would propose such an idea. They argued that Kevorkian's ideas were a violation of the Hippocratic Oath, even if he never did such a deadly experiment.

It was not long before Kevorkian's colleagues began to refer to him as "Doctor Death," a nickname that stayed with him the rest of his life.

Doctor Death's reputation for unorthodox medical and academic theories caused him professional problems during the 1960s. Following the publication of his idea to experiment on death row inmates, Kevorkian was terminated from his internship at the

University of Michigan. Although the termination was a setback, Kevorkian sojourned on as he always did and landed another internship at Pontiac General Hospital. It was while he was at Pontiac General that Kevorkian began a new experimentation with the dead.

While Kevorkian was in Korea, one of the major problems that he saw firsthand concerning wounded soldiers was the availability of blood for transfusions. He began to consider using the blood of corpses for transfusions to save the living. Although the idea may seem a bit macabre at first, it is really no different than harvesting organs from the dead for transplant, after all blood is essentially an organ.

The problem is that blood coagulates very quickly, making it unusable. There is also the question of the deceased's health history—without proper tests it would be unknown if the donor had any critical blood borne diseases.

As Kevorkian ruminated on this idea, he came across some research from the 1930s Soviet Union where doctors claimed to have successfully done several such transfusions. Intrigued, Kevorkian began doing transfusions on corpses and using himself as the living guinea pig. Although the process was difficult, it was somewhat successful, enough so that he published his findings in an article titled, "Transfusion of Human Corpse Blood without Additives," in *Transfusion* journal in 1964.

The publication of the article silenced some of Kevorkian's critics, but it also put more pressure on the controversial doctor's life.

The experiments with corpse blood transfusions also left Kevorkian with Hepatitis C, which would later contribute to his death.

The Doctor of Death in Action

Although Kevorkian had earned the reputation as a controversial yet gifted researcher by the 1960s, his polarizing personality often left him jobless. By the early 1980s, he had burned several bridges in the Michigan medical community and occasionally found himself homeless, living in his car and relying on the generosity of his friends and family.

But it was during the 1980s when Kevorkian transformed from an obscure medical researcher with some fringe ideas to the face of the right to die movement in the United States.

Always one to keep abreast of current affairs in both politics and medicine, Kevorkian learned that the Netherlands began to allow terminally ill patients the right to assisted suicide during the 1980s. The news of the Dutch law gave new life to Kevorkian and his career. He began researching both the science behind and the ethical ramifications of assisted suicide for terminally ill patients and published his ideas in a series of academic articles.

Although Kevorkian proved to still be a polarizing figure in the medical community, he found greater acceptance for his ideas on assisted suicide and he also began to acquire allies in politics.

Once he became convinced that a terminally ill patient had the right to die, Kevorkian then began to devise ways in which the theory could be put into action. After doing some experiments, the Doctor of Death devised an invention he called the "thanatron." Thantron is a Greek word that in English roughly translates to "instrument of death." The patient in question would be hooked up to the thanatron with needles and IVs and then given a series of three drugs: saline, a painkiller, and then a fatal dose of potassium chloride.

With his efficient instrument of death, Kevorkian only needed a volunteer.

Kevorkian did not have to look long or far to find a volunteer. By 1990, the Doctor of Death was well known in Michigan for his views on euthanasia and assisted suicide and, as noted above, had begun to amass support with various political and advocacy groups.

One of the groups that supported Kevorkian's ideas was the Hemlock Society.

The Hemlock Society, named for the drug that the philosopher Socrates took to end his life, was a national right to die organization that formed in 1980. By the time that Kevorkian had invented his thanatron and was looking for the first volunteer, the organization was quite familiar with the Doctor of Death and his philosophies.

Kevorkian's first volunteer was a fifty-four-year-old Michigander member of the Hemlock Society named Janet Adkins.

In 1990, Adkins was suffering from early onset Alzheimer's disease and wanted to end her life in the most painless way possible. Members of the Michigan Hemlock Society connected her to Kevorkian and after the two met to discuss her options and what the Doctor of Death could do, she decided to be his first volunteer.

Adkins and Kevorkian met in a park and then walked to his van where the thanatron was hooked up and ready to go. After he made sure that Adkins was comfortable, Kevorkian hooked the IV up to her arm and then had her press the button that administered the drugs.

Janet Adkins drifted off into eternal sleep within a matter of minutes.

Once the details of the assisted suicide were made public, Kevorkian was charged with murder, but the charges were quickly dropped due to vagueness in Michigan law concerning assisted suicide.

The assisted suicide of Janet Adkins made Jack Kevorkian a well-known public figure, but it also brought the doctor immense scrutiny and legal problems.

Legal Problems for the Doctor of Death

Although Kevorkian avoided prosecution in the assisted suicide of Janet Adkins, lawmakers and the courts in Michigan did not give up their crusade against the Doctor of Death so easily. The first blow came in 1991 when the state of Michigan revoked his medical license. The move was more symbolic than anything. At that time, Kevorkian had not worked in a hospital setting for some time and instead derived most of his income from donations and "death counseling."

As long as Kevorkian could continue helping people with their end of life decisions and providing the thanatron as an alternative to those who chose assisted suicide, then the Doctor of Death could make a living.

But in 1991 a judge issued a legal injunction against Kevorkian using the thanatron.

The injunction, though, proved to be only a minor stumbling block for the right to die advocate. Not long after the injunction was issued, Kevorkian invented a new death machine he called the "mercitron." The mercitron operated under very different scientific principles than the thanatron. Instead of killing the patient with a lethal drug cocktail, the merictron, translated approximately as "mercy machine," killed the patient with a lethal dose of carbon dioxide delivered via a mask.

The rebellious and clever Kevorkian had essentially waved a metaphorical finger at government of Michigan and the lawmakers were not happy!

In 1992, the Michigan state legislature passed a law outlawing any form of assisted suicide, no matter the device used. Anyone caught violating the law was subject to murder charges.

Kevorkian was a true believer in the philosophies of assisted suicide and the right to die, but he was also an intelligent realist, so he decided to hire an attorney before he moved forward. He retained the colorful and sometimes controversial Michigan attorney, Jeff Fieger, as his criminal defense attorney and public relations guru throughout the 1990s.

Fieger, who had established a nice practice for himself after earning his J.D. from the Detroit College of Law in 1979, had his hands full with Kevorkian. After Kevorkian helped a terminally ill patient commit suicide in 1993, the Doctor of Death was charged with murder. Fieger successful defended Kevorkian in his 1994 trial and three other times throughout the 1990s with a record of three acquittals and one mistrial. Fieger stated that Kevorkian helped over 130 terminally ill patients commit suicide during this period using both the thanatron and the mericitron.

Kevorkian became a fixture in the American news cycle during the 1990s and his fame even bled into the realm of pop culture. The Doctor of Death seemed to relish the post-trial interviews he gave to the press, so much so that Fieger more than once told him to "shut up" while he was giving an interview.

But the fame that Kevorkian attained performing assisted suicides eventually went to his head and developed into hubris.

In November 1998, Kevorkian set up an assisted suicide for a fifty-two-year-old man who suffered from ALS. Instead of doing the procedure in privacy, Kevorkian invited reporters from the weekly news program *60 Minutes* to observe and tape the suicide. Once the authorities in Michigan saw the tape, they charged Kevorkian with a plethora of crimes, the most serious being second-degree murder.

The Doctor of Death would have to face another Michigan jury for his assisted suicide activities, but this time he would do so without Fieger.

In a move that he later regretted, Kevorkian defended himself on the charges and not surprisingly was convicted of second-degree murder on March 26, 1999.

The Doctor of Death's career was over, at least temporarily.

Kevorkian was given a sentence of ten to twenty-five years in prison and promptly sent to the Michigan Department of Corrections where he spent the next eight years with some of the most violent criminals in the state. His time in prison, was for the most part, uneventful. He kept to himself and got along with the other inmates and occasionally gave interviews to the media. After being denied parole a couple of times, the Doctor of Death was finally released from prison in June 2007.

Like many who serve years in prison, the experience, combined with his advanced age, seemed to have mellowed Kevorkian. He was barred from assisting in any suicides, even in places where it was now legal, and so instead spent his time lecturing on the benefits of the right to die. After suffering from Hepatitis C he contracted from his blood transfusion experiments in the 1960s, the Doctor of Death finally met the Grim Reaper on June 3, 2011, at the age of eighty-three.

Jack Kevorkian's Influence on America

Today, few Americans under the age of thirty-five do not know who Jack Kevorkian was. The elderly glasses-wearing Kevorkian proved to be ample fodder for comedians during the 1990s and a number of heavy metal bands also referred to the Doctor of Death and his endeavors in a number of songs. The premium cable channel, HBO, produced a movie in 2010 titled, *You Don't Know Jack*, starring screen legend Al Pacino as Kevorkian. The film renewed interest in Jack Kevorkian and brought his story to a whole new generation of people.

Beyond the influence Kevorkian had on American pop culture, his most enduring legacy concerns how he changed many people's attitude about assisted suicide.

Since Kevorkian's crusade of assisted suicide in the 1990s, several states have legalized the practice and others are considering legislation. The topic continues to be polarizing and will not go away anytime soon, but because of Kevorkian the right to die movement now has a legitimate place in the American political discourse.

"Dr. Jack Kevorkian didn't seek out history," said Jeff Fieger about his former client. "But he made history."

CHAPTER 6:
The Saga of the Menendez Brothers

Murder is about the most horrific crime a person can commit and in particular patricide and matricide, the killing of one's father and mother respectively, are considered especially odious to most people. There is no doubt that when we hear about someone who killed his or her parents, we feel a little more sick than usual.

Despite society's deep aversion to parental murder, it has been not that uncommon throughout history. Perhaps the most well-known story of parental murder is the ancient Greek play *Oedipus Rex*. In *Oedipus*, the titular character unknowingly kills his father and equally unknowingly takes his own mother as his wife. The fictional tale provides an extreme case of parental murder, but many more cases are known throughout history.

There are several documented cases, from Persia to France, of ambitious young princes killing their fathers in order to become king of certain realms. In modern times, there have also been numerous documented cases of parental murder, but the motivations have differed somewhat from the earlier examples.

Many cases of parental murder in modern times involve victims of abuse—teenagers who have been sexually and/or physically abused by one or both of their parents. These kids feel they have no recourse other than to lash out violently against the very people who were supposed to protect them. These are the most tragic cases, but probably more common are those who kill their parents out of greed.

You do not have to peruse news archives very long to find articles about people who killed one or both of their parents for the riches of an inheritance.

During the early 1990s, Americans were glued to their television sets as they watched the trial of two brothers, Erik and Lyle Menendez, who faced a possible death sentence for the murders of both of their parents. The police investigation of the brothers and the trial saw many twists and turns. The brothers claimed they killed due to abuse, but the jury believed they did so out of greed.

The American Dream

The tragic story of the Menendez family began in the late 1950s on the island of Cuba. In the midst of Fidel Castro's takeover of the island that turned Cuba into a communist dictatorship and the subsequent reign of terror that he imposed on his political enemies, a sixteen-year-old boy named Jose Menendez fled with thousands of other Cubans to the safe confines of Miami, Florida. Once in the United States, Jose worked hard, completed high school, and earned a swimming scholarship to the University of

Southern Illinois.

When Jose arrived in Carbondale, Illinois, to begin his education, he was quickly faced with culture shock and home-sickness. Although he made friends easily and did well in his coursework and swimming, the cold winters and lack of Latin culture proved to be a difficult adjustment for the young Cuban expatriate.

But Jose soon found a friend to help him navigate through the nuances of Middle America in the early 1960s.

Jose met Mary Louise "Kitty" Andersen on the campus of the University of Southern Illinois. At first glance the two seemed like an unlikely pair—Kitty was born and raised in working class suburban Chicago family—but they quickly fell in love and eloped in 1963.

Shortly after their marriage, the couple moved to the New York City area to start a family.

Things were not easy at first for the couple as Jose had difficulties finding work as an accountant. Despite the problems, Jose eventually found work and then their first son, Joseph Lyle, was born in 1968. In 1970 Kitty gave birth to their youngest son, Erik Galen. During the 1970s Kitty devoted most of her time to raising the couple's two sons, while Jose earned a reputation as an excellent accountant.

Jose Menendez had realized the American dream.

But beyond the façade of a successful, all-American family, there were fissures turning into cracks.

Jose began cheating on Kitty and eventually took mistresses whom he lavished with expensive gifts and apartments. At first, Jose tried to be discreet with his indiscretions, but over time he became more flagrant with his affairs. The result was that the Menendez home became the site of numerous arguments, confrontations, and general turmoil that Erik and Lyle witnessed. Kitty began to drink for solace and Jose spent less time at home.

It seemed to be a marriage doomed to divorce.

But in the late 1980s, the marriage received a reprieve of sorts when Jose became the CEO of the film studio and home video company LIVE Entertainment. The position meant that Jose and his family would have to move to southern California, which they did in 1987.

At first, the move seemed beneficial for the Menendez family, but within two years the parents were dead and the sons were on trial for their murders.

Erik and Lyle Menendez

Erik and Lyle Menendez's early lives can be described as unimpressive at best. The aphorism, "the apple doesn't fall far from the tree" clearly did not apply in their case. Neither of the brothers seemed to be imbued with their father's intelligence, ambition, and charisma and if they were not born into a life of privilege, it would be difficult to see them doing anything special with their lives.

Erik's grades in high school were average, but he showed no real academic interests or ambitions. He did excel in sports, especially tennis, which is how he chose to spend most of his time as a teenager. About the only intellectual interest that Erik displayed was when he wrote a rough draft of a screenplay. Ironically, the plot of the play concerned an heir killing his father in order to gain the family inheritance.

While Erik was an underachiever, Lyle was truly a disappointment to his parents.

Lyle's grades in high school were nominally better than Erik's, but it was his father's money and influence that landed him a spot at Princeton University. As an Ivy League school, Princeton's academic standards are extremely rigorous and its code of conduct is very strict.

Lyle failed at Princeton in both of those areas.

Choosing to socialize and party instead of study, Lyle's grades suffered in his first semester. Instead of choosing to dedicate himself to improving his grades through study and hard work, Lyle decided to take the easy way out by plagiarizing a term paper. The accusations of plagiarism were never followed up by the university, though, because Lyle decided to call it quits and move back to southern California.

Jose felt that something drastic needed to be done in order to set

Lyle on the right path. After Lyle came home to live with his parents in California, he worked briefly for his father at LIVE Entertainment. Jose thought that the job could possibly interest Lyle and give him some goals to work toward. He also hoped that Lyle would excel in the position and possibly carry on in the business that made him so much money. The job was simple; essentially it just consisted of some basic clerical and assistant duties, but Lyle proved to be equally inept at that position and did not get along with his coworkers, so Jose was forced to fire him.

Lyle was also arrested for, but not convicted of, breaking into a neighbor's home when the Menendez family lived in Calabasas, California. Although the burglary charges against him were dropped, the stigma proved to be too much for the family, so Jose moved them to Beverly Hills, which was the home where the murders took place.

Besides his ethical and legal problems, Lyle was known to have a violent temper and was said to abuse his girlfriends. Clearly, Lyle was the more explosive of the two brothers and as was revealed later at their trials, he was the one calling the shots for the duo.

Massacre at the Menendez Home

The late summer day of August 20, 1989, began just like any other day at the Menendez mansion. Jose and Kitty had gone shark fishing in the Pacific Ocean the day before with some friends, so they decided to stay in that evening and take it easy. The couple slept in that day, did some work around the house, and then settled in during the early evening hours. Jose and Kitty decided to spend the evening in their den watching some movies.

Movie night ended tragically for Jose and Kitty Menendez.

The Neighbors reported hearing a series of loud bangs around ten p.m. that evening, which was uncommon in the normally quiet, affluent neighborhood. Despite clearly hearing sounds that were out of the ordinary, no neighbors called the police because they later said they thought it was either fireworks or a car backfiring.

The reality is that Jose and Kitty were being brutally murdered.

When the police arrived at the scene, the den was covered in blood. Jose lay dead on the couch in front of the television with half his head blown off from the blast of a twelve gauge shotgun. The killers surprised the entertainment executive—he never had a chance.

The police surmised that Kitty was sleeping on the couch next to Jose when he was shot. After the fatal shot was fired, Kitty woke up and tried to run out the front door but was shot several times and killed in the hallway.

Both Jose and Kitty were shot in their kneecaps, which led some detectives early in the investigation to think that the murders may have been related to organized crime. Perhaps Jose had an affair with the wrong man's wife or maybe he was involved in a shady business deal with an underworld figure, so a hit was put out on him. The "kneecapping" of both victims seemed to point toward a mob hit, but the more the investigators looked at the case and the background of the Menendez family, the more Erik and Lyle looked good for the murders.

When interviewed by Beverly Hills detectives, Erik and Lyle stated that they were at a movie on the evening of the murders and then met some friends at a bar. Their friends from the bar were able to corroborate that part of their alibi, but the brothers were each other's alibi for the movie, so the police were initially suspicious.

Erik and Lyle returned to the family home around midnight when a frantic Lyle called 911 and said, "Somebody killed my parents!"

Although the initial investigation focused on the Menendez brothers, a number of factors delayed the arrest of Erik and Lyle. For some reason, neither Erik's or Lyle's hands were tested for gunshot residue on the night of the murders. A positive test would have shown the police that both men had recently fired a gun and would have been a solid piece of evidence against them. The shotguns used to kill Jose and Kitty were never recovered, but it was later revealed in court that the brothers dumped the guns in garbage cans in different locations around Los Angeles.

The security, or lack thereof, of the Menendez home also proved to be a factor that clouded the investigation. Jose frequently turned the security off in the home, which would have allowed the killers to quietly slip into the home undetected. Jose had one of his cars recently stolen from the front driveway of the home because he also tended to leave the gate around the home unlocked. The security issues at the Menendez home caused some investigators to posit that the killers may have been professional thieves who killed Jose and Kitty to eliminate any witnesses.

But the majority of the investigators working the case knew that professional burglars rarely kill people in cold blood and they almost never use twelve gauges.

The focus of the investigation turned toward Erik and Lyle once more.

Living Large

As the police investigation into the murders of Jose and Kitty Menendez began to focus more and more on Erik and Lyle, the two brothers began to display their lack of maturity and common sense. A seasoned criminal in their position would generally choose to keep a low profile in order to allay any suspicions by the authorities before he or she would collect the inheritance.

But Erik and Lyle were no seasoned criminals, nor were they very bright.

Almost immediately after the murder of their parents, the brothers moved out of the family mansion and into separate penthouse apartments in the Los Angeles beachfront neighborhood of Marina Del Rey.

The two brothers indulged by buying Rolex watches and expensive cars, and were seen around town at the most expensive restaurants. Lyle bought a restaurant and Erik took tennis lessons from a professional in order to realize his dream of becoming a professional tennis player.

Erik and Lyle also traveled extensively, both alone and separately, around the United States, Europe, and the Caribbean.

Los Angeles County prosecutors estimated that the Menendez brothers spent about one million dollars of their family's fortune in the six months after their parents' murders. Although the brothers were doing nothing illegal by living large after their parents' murders, their behavior was later used in court against them as the primary motive for the murders. Erik and Lyle were two spoiled, lazy kids who could not wait to get their hands on the family fortune, the prosecutors argued.

But as Erik and Lyle spent their blood money, the investigators were putting together a case for murder.

The Arrest and Trial of the Menendez Brothers

The brutal murders that the Menendez brothers committed apparently weighed more heavily on the conscience of Erik that it did Lyle's. In early November 1989, just over two months after the murders of Jose and Kitty, Erik went to see Beverly Hills psychologist L. Jerome Oziel. The session was like no other for Oziel because his patient confessed to killing his parents!

Although Oziel kept the doctor-client confidentiality immediately after the session, the meeting set off a chain of events that resulted in the arrests of the Menendez brothers. Once Lyle learned of his brother's confession to Oziel, he threatened the psychologist, which eventually led to him violating the doctor-client privilege. Feeling trapped between the doctor-client privilege and threats by a killer, Oziel eventually went to the Los Angeles County District Attorney's office.

But before Oziel said anything to the Los Angeles County prosecutors, his ex-girlfriend, Judalon Smyth, who overheard Erik's session with Oziel through a closed door, told of the confession to the police.

The confession was just the last piece in a puzzle of circumstantial evidence that clearly showed Erik and Lyle to be the killers of their parents. Besides the lavish spending immediately after the murders and the confession to the psychologist, the Beverly Hills Police learned that the brothers deleted Jose's will from the family computer.

Arrest warrants for the charge of first degree murder were issued for the arrests of the Menendez brothers. Lyle was quickly picked up on March 8, 1990, but Erik was in Israel at a tennis tournament. Instead of going on the run, Erik decided to fly back to Los Angeles three days later and face justice with his brother.

Due to the severe nature of the crimes and the fact that the brothers still had immense resources at their disposal, the Menendez brothers were denied bail and remanded to a protective custody unit in the Los Angeles County Jail.

Most importantly for Erik and Lyle, they were placed in different cell blocks.

The accommodations were quite a shock to the two young men who were used to the finer things in life. Gone were their Rolexes, sports cars, and pretty women. Instead, the two were forced to wear orange county jail jumpsuits, eat bologna sandwiches, and shower in front of guards. The lifestyle that the two brothers tried so desperately to attain was suddenly taken from them.

And if things did not go their way in trial, they faced losing those things for the rest of their lives!

Most murder cases in the United States take several months to make it to trial. There are several pre-trial motions and hearings that take place and sometimes the jury selection can take several weeks. The time that it takes to bring a case to trial is often criticized, but both the defense and prosecution take advantage of the time because a lot of time and resources are needed to either defend or prosecute a major case.

It took about three years for the Menendez brothers' trial to begin.

One of the primary factors that delayed the trial so long were the numerous motions concerning the admissibility of Erik's confession to his psychologist. The defense argued that the confession, which was taped by Ozeil, could not be used in court because it was a violation of the doctor-patient privilege protected under California law. The California Supreme Court eventually ruled that some of the tapes could be used in trial, but not the part where Erik confessed to the murders.

Once the ruling on the tapes was made, it was time for the trial to begin.

Because the trial involved patricide and a story of privilege gone awry, Erik and Lyle's trial garnered immense media attention and public interest, which seemed to favor the brothers. Erik hired high-profile defense attorney Leslie Abramson, who dutifully gave press conferences and interviews nearly every day in order to get her client's defense into the public.

Leslie Abramson decided to try the case in the media.

Although the brothers were tried at the same time in the same courtroom, two different juries were assembled—one for each defendant. The unusual circumstances of having two juries, but essentially only one trial, only seemed to add to the already bizarre case.

But things got even stranger when the brothers took the stand in their own defense.

Erik and Lyle shocked the country when they admitted to carrying out the brutal murders, but they argued that the homicides were carried out in self-defense. Often crying, the brothers testified that Jose had abused them since they were children—physically, sexually, and mentally—and that Kitty was an alcoholic who acquiesced to the situation in order to keep up the façade of a normal, healthy family.

After months of testimony, both juries announced that they were hopelessly deadlocked. The judge declared mistrials for both Menendez brothers, but the celebrations would have to wait because Los Angeles County District Attorney Gil Garcetti stated in a post-trial press conference that he would retry the Menendez brothers.

The defense and prosecution of the second Menendez brothers trial were essentially the same, but the defense was hampered my one major difference—the judge barred cameras from the courtroom.

The case could no longer be tried in the media.

The result was that Erik and Lyle Menendez were convicted of first degree murder and given life in prison without the possibility of parole on July 2, 1996.

Although the Menendez brothers will never again see the outside of a prison, they continue to make news from behind bars. Both men have married while in prison and Lyle even divorced his first wife and remarried in 2003. Since California law prohibits inmates with life sentences from having conjugal visits, the level of contact that the brothers have with their wives is minimal.

But perhaps the biggest punishment that the Menendez brothers have to endure for their horrific crimes is the forced separation from each other. The two brothers that once did everything together, including killing their parents, have been housed in separate prisons since their convictions, which will probably remain the case for the rest of their lives.

CHAPTER 7:
The Murder of the Wilson Family

Unfortunately, crime has become a major factor concerning how we live in modern society. It dictates how we interact with others and where we live. The growth of major American suburbs over the last fifty years can be directly traced to crime—as crime rates increased during the 1960s and '70s, more and more people moved from the inner cities to the suburbs.

But the "good" neighborhoods are not always immune to crime.

Crime in the suburbs and wealthier neighborhoods is often done for the same reasons as in the inner city: greed, domestic violence, and drug addiction are all reasons that fuel crime in all socioeconomic levels.

Then there are the senseless crimes—murders committed by individuals from good homes for no discernable reason other than for the thrill of it.

The case of Nathan Leopold and Richard Loeb—two bright young men from affluent families who killed a boy in 1924 just to see if they could commit the "perfect crime"—is one of the most famous cases of wealthy thrill killers from the annals of crime history. The

Columbine High School massacre perpetrated by Dylan Klebold and Eric Harris in 1999 is another example of two young men from good families who decided to play god.

Murder can and does happen in the suburbs and sometimes it is done for no other reason than the thrill of it.

On January 3, 1997, over two years before the Columbine High School massacre, four members of a family in the affluent Seattle suburb of Bellevue, Washington, were brutally murdered, three of them in their own home. When the residents of the Seattle area learned of the brutal quadruple murder, they were shocked and frightened, but they became even more so when they learned who had perpetrated the crimes and why.

A Gothic Mystery

In early 1997, the Wilsons were just like most other suburban American families. Fifty-two-year-old father William and forty-six-year-old mother Rose worked hard to provide plenty of material comforts for their two children, seventeen-year-old Julia and twenty-year-old Kimberly. The family had its ups and downs, but nothing out of the ordinary. Kimberly, who still lived at home at the time of the murders, went through a rebellious phase in high school, but had since moved past that and appeared ready to transition into adult life. No one in the family was known to be involved in drug use or criminal activity, which is why friends and family of the Wilsons were perplexed when they learned of the murders.

The mystery began when two boys playing in a park near the Wilson home discovered the body of a young woman on the morning of January 4, 1997. Bellevue Police homicide detective Jeff Gomes responded to the scene, and, after looking at the victim's ID, he learned that she was a local resident named Kimberly Wilson. Following police protocol, Gomes went to the Wilson home to tell the parents the horrible news.

Gomes was braced to tell Kimberly's family the horrible news. He was a veteran homicide detective, so he knew how emotional the situation could be and he also knew that every situation was different. Because of his experience, he would mentally prepare himself each time he notified the family of a homicide victim.

There was no way he could prepare himself for what he found at the Wilson home.

When he arrived at the Wilson home, no one answered the door, which was unlocked, so he went inside, identifying himself as a police officer. When he went inside and turned on the lights, the twenty-three-year police veteran was horrified at what he found.

The walls and floors were covered in blood!

As Gomes made his way throughout the house, he came to the master bedroom where he found the mangled bodies of William and Rose. The couple had literally had their heads bashed in so badly that they were unrecognizable. Julia was discovered stabbed and beaten to death. Gomes and the other investigators surmised that the killers surprised the couple and then attacked Julia, who tried to fend off the attacker, or attackers, as evidenced by defensive wounds on her hands.

It was clear that Kimberly's murder was connected to the killings of her family members, but detectives were at a complete loss as to who would commit such horrendous crimes.

There were no signs of sexual assault on any of the female members of the Wilson household and nothing valuable appeared to be missing from the home. Theories about the murders began circulating almost immediately throughout the Seattle area. Some thought that it was part of an organized crime hit, while others believed that it was a case of mistaken identity.

Gomes quickly wrote off such theories because he found no evidence of criminal activity with any members of the family, and the murders, although extremely brutal, did not look like the work of a professional.

But with anything this big, secrets are hard to keep.

The investigators working on the Wilson case followed up every lead, no matter how outlandish, with nothing to show for their efforts. Eventually, more credible tips started coming in that told the detectives to focus on the local Goth scene and two young men in particular, David Anderson and Alex Baranyi.

In 1997, David Anderson and Alex Baranyi were two slackers with no real goals or ambitions for the future. Baranyi was described by friends and acquaintances as a socially awkward loner who had no real friends other than Anderson. It was not entirely his fault, though, as he found it difficult to put down any roots during his adolescence. Baranyi's parent's divorced when he was young and afterwards, he often moved between his two parents and the locales of Pennsylvania and Seattle. It was during his time in the Seattle area in the mid-1990s that he met David Anderson.

In many ways, Anderson was the polar opposite of Baranyi. Anderson was a somewhat physically imposing former high school wrestler who was known to take over conversations through a combination of sheer force and charm. Because Anderson possessed a certain level of charisma, he was reasonably well-liked by other kids his age, including girls, and got along fairly well with his teachers and other adults.

Despite the personality differences between Baranyi and Anderson, they shared the same interest in the Goth subculture.

Over the last two decades, the Goth subculture has acquired a bad reputation. The 1996 "vampire clan" murders in Eustice, Florida and the Columbine High School massacre were perpetrated by young people on the periphery of the Goth scene, but the reality is that there are tens of thousands more people who take part in the subculture that never commit a violent act.

Part of the reason for the Goth subculture's negative publicity, besides the above mentioned murders, is the fact that the style is centered on dark and mysterious subject matter. Goths often enjoy dressing in dark, Victorian-era inspired clothing and the music they listen to often deals with dark subject matters. With that said, the Goth subculture is not monolithic and there are several sub-groupings. Some Goths focus their energy more on dark literature by authors such as Mary Shelly and Bram Stoker, while others are more attracted to the subculture for the industrial-techno music.

Anderson and Baranyi wore black, listened to the industrial style of music popular with many Goths, and played role playing games about vampires. The two young men associated with others in the Goth scene from the Bellevue area, including Kimberly Wilson, but began to drift away from the scene when they both dropped out of high school.

The two lived on the good graces of their parents and instead of spending their days looking for work, they would spend all night at twenty-four hour restaurants like Denny's playing vampire role-playing games.

Friends of the duo said that they had a difficult time separating fantasy from reality. Anderson and Baranyi began to collect knives, swords, and other exotic weapons and tell any who would listen how they planned to use the weapons to dispatch people in the future. What disturbed some of their friends most was not necessarily that they talked of killing, but that they talked of killing people randomly and just for the thrill.

Despite the extremely violent talk by the duo, most of their friends thought it was just a combination of teenage angst and a false sense of bravado. They may have been confused and slightly disturbed, their friends reasoned, but they were not cold-blooded killers.

There were other signs of problems beyond the duo's growing isolation and fascination with violence.

Baranyi had an assault report filed against him by his ex-girlfriend, Dawn Kindschi, not long before the Wilson family murder, but the report was not followed through, so the young Goth was never punished. Kindschi was truly afraid of and for Baranyi.

"Sometimes I thought he might be sort of suicidal," Kindschi later told a reporter.

Not long after the Wilson family murders, acquaintances and friends of Anderson's and Baranyi's told the Bellevue Police that there were numerous reasons why those two should be investigated. Before Gomes and the other homicide investigators could do a thorough background check on Anderson and Baranyi, one of Baranyi's friends came into the police station with an incredible story.

Every Man for Himself

Baranyi's friend told Gomes that Anderson and Baranyi simply killed the Wilson family for fun. Although they both knew Kimberly, they were for the most part, indifferent toward her; she was just the unfortunate victim of a twisted game.

The information was not enough to obtain arrest warrants for

Baranyi and Anderson, but it did fill in a lot of holes in the investigation and it gave Gomes an advantage when he interviewed Baranyi. Since the information came from one of Baranyi's friends and Baranyi was determined to be the weaker of the duo, Gomes decided to go hard after Baranyi. At first, Baranyi offered Bellevue homicide investigators a weak alibi, but once that was picked apart, he decided to confess and turn on his best friend.

Baranyi said that he and Anderson found their lives in a "rut", which they thought they could get out of by committing murder. According to Baranyi, Kimberly Wilson was a target of opportunity—since they knew her, they were able to lure her to a more deserted area of the park where they could then carry out their nefarious plan. After killing Kimberly, the two then went to her family's home to continue the carnage with a sword and baseball bat.

Gomes and the other investigators were disturbed to learn that two seemingly normal young men living in their community could kill four people just for fun. A forensic team thoroughly searched Baranyi's apartment, which later determined that the soles of a pair of his boots matched a bloody pattern found at the Wilson home.

There was other physical and circumstantial evidence that tied Baranyi to the murders. Some of William Wilson's DNA was found on a CD player in Baranyi's apartment and witnesses reported that

Baranyi talked about killing the Wilson family over a year before the murders.

Baranyi's guilt in the Wilson murders looked unequivocal, but Anderson's involvement was not so clear.

When the police questioned Anderson, he stated that he had nothing to do with the murders and that he heard Baranyi was the sole culprit. As an alibi, Anderson said that he was driving his girlfriend's father's car around aimlessly all night. The alibi was pretty weak to begin with; he could offer the police no receipts from any gas stations and there was no one who claimed to have seen Anderson driving around. The Bellevue homicide detectives did not need to dig very deep to destroy Anderson's alibi. When they asked Anderson's girlfriend's father about the suspect using his car, he refuted that story and said the car was parked at his house all night. Anderson was eventually charged with the murders, although the prosecutors had a lot less evidence to present to a jury.

The Murder Trials of David Anderson and Alex Baranyi

By the time the two "thicker than thieves" friends, David Anderson and Alex Baranyi, went to trial in 1998 for the murders of the Wilson family, they were bitter enemies. First Baranyi confessed to the murders and implicated Anderson while denying any involvement, but Anderson said Baranyi confessed the crimes to him. Like any murder trial, the Wilson family murder case was complete with several pre-trial motions that took place over the period of several months.

One of the first pre-trial motions that Anderson's defense team filed was to have the two defendants tried separately. The judge granted the request, which was seen as a victory for Anderson, who had much less forensic and circumstantial evidence stacked against him.

After the trials of the two defendants were severed, Baranyi's lawyers argued that his confession was obtained improperly because he was not informed properly of his right to counsel. The judge agreed, but there was still a mountain of evidence against Baranyi.

The bloody boot print and William Wilson's DNA, which was discovered in Baranyi's apartment, were still used as pieces of the puzzle against Baranyi. Then there were the numerous statements he made to his friends about violence in general and specifically against the Wilson family.

The evidence was enough for a jury to convict Baranyi of first degree murder in late 1998. Alex Baranyi was sentenced to life without the possibility of parole in the Washington State Department of Corrections.

Whereas the case against Baranyi was considered a legal "slam dunk," King County prosecutors had a much more difficult time proving their case against David Anderson. There was no real physical evidence linking Anderson to any of the murders, but the prosecutors put a number of witnesses on the stand—more than in Baranyi's trial—who testified that Anderson boasted about the murders. A medical examiner also testified that due to the number of people killed in one location and the fact that multiple weapons were used, more than one perpetrator was responsible for the murder.

Anderson's trial resulted in a mistrial when the jury could not come to a verdict. Undeterred, the prosecutors retried the case and earned a conviction in 1999. Anderson, like Baranyi, was also sentenced to life in prison without parole.

The two will now have plenty of time to play vampire role-playing games.

CHAPTER 8:
The Robert Blake Murder Trial

In 2001, Americans were surprised to learn that the wife of well-known television and movie star, Robert Blake, was murdered on the streets of Los Angeles. It was a surprise partly because it is relatively rare for spouses of the rich and famous to become murder victims.

It was also interesting because Robert Blake is known for his many roles as tough guys.

During the 1950s and '60s, Blake often played gangsters and outlaws, but he is probably best known for the lead role in the 1970s television police drama, *Baretta*. In *Baretta,* Blake played a plain-clothes, unconventional detective who was willing to bend the rules and use violence when necessary.

Blake became a millionaire playing violent men, but on the evening of May 4, 2001, violence became a reality in his life when his wife, Bonnie Lee Bakley, was shot to death outside of a Los Angeles restaurant.

Bonnie Lee Bakley

To say Bonnie Lee Bakley was an interesting woman would be an understatement. Born to an upper middle class family in 1956, Bakley dropped out of high school at the age of sixteen and moved to New York City to pursue a career in the entertainment industry. Bakley was unable to find work in her desired profession, but she did discover a particular aptitude at taking advantage of men.

The attractive and charismatic woman would seduce men through newspaper personals and then fleece them of their money. She would feign interest in any man that answered her ads and then would tell them that she needed money for something important like an operation. Bakley used the money to buy properties in Memphis, Tennessee and Los Angles, which supported her financially while she pursued her entertainment career. The scam actually worked quite well and was able to give Bakley a lifestyle that would have normally been out of her reach.

Ultimately, Bakley could never find work in the entertainment industry, but she was able to become the companion of several entertainers. She used the money made off of her real estate investments to move in the upper socioeconomic level.

Bakley dated Jerry "The Killer" Lewis when she lived in Memphis during the 1990s; but the relationship ended when she gave birth to a child that she claimed was his, but turned out to be another man's. Undeterred, she then moved to Los Angeles where she dated a number of celebrities, most notably Gary Busey, Christian

Brando, and finally Robert Blake.

In 2000, well into her forties, Bakley gave birth to a daughter she named Rose. At first, she thought Brando was the father, but a paternity test later revealed that the sixty-six-year-old Blake was the father. Although Blake had his doubts about Bakley—she had been married nine times before Blake and had three other children—he decided to marry her in late 2000.

Needless to say, the marriage was far from perfect.

The Murder

On the evening of May 4, 2001, Blake and Bakley went out for dinner to Vitello's Restaurant in the Studio City neighborhood of Los Angeles, California. Blake drove the couple and parked on a side street about a block from the restaurant. By all accounts, the meal was uneventful, Blake paid the bill, and the couple left. Blake returned a few minutes later to claim a gun he had left at the desk while they had their meal.

While Blake was in the restaurant alone, Bakley was shot and killed as she sat in the car.

When the police arrived at the scene, they were immediately faced with a number of problems. There were no eye or ear witnesses to the shooting and no bullet casings left behind.

The police were immediately suspicious of the situation for a number of reasons.

Although Los Angeles is a city with its share of crime, most of the crime is relegated to certain sections of the city, which do not include Studio City. Yes, random crimes do unfortunately happen every day across the United States, but they are usually committed for some discernable reason. Bakley's purse was not stolen and there appeared to be no struggle, as if she knew her killer and the missing bullet casings suggested a hit done by a professional.

An investigation into Blake's background revealed the unconventional nature of the marriage he had with Bakley. Before they married, Blake made Bakley sign an agreement that if one of them were to file for divorce, the other would retain custody of their child. There were also rumors of infidelity and abuse.

The gun that Blake claimed to have left in Vittello's was given a ballistics test, but it was determined not to be the weapon that killed Bakley. Despite this perceived setback, the Los Angeles Police were convinced that Blake was the killer.

Unable to find any forensic evidence against Blake, the police widened their investigative net to include all known associates of the actor. Eventually, they located two former stuntmen who claimed that Blake offered to pay them to murder his wife.

The statements would be enough for an arrest, but would they hold up in trial?

Baretta Goes on Trial

Despite a lack of physical or eyewitness evidence, the Los Angeles County District Attorney's office thought that they had enough to convict Robert Blake of murder. Their case would rest on a combination of circumstantial and "snitch" testimony. The lead prosecutor in the case, Shellie Samuels, admitted in an interview on the television program *48 Hours Investigates* that they had no eyewitnesses or forensic/physical evidence against Blake. Despite those obvious problems, the Los Angeles County District Attorney's office decided to charge Blake with one count of first degree murder and two counts of solicitation to murder on April 22, 2002.

In a surprise move to many, including Blake, the prosecutors listed the murder charge as taking place under "special circumstances," which meant that Blake could face the death penalty under California law if convicted.

Along with Blake, his bodyguard, Earle Caldwell, was charged with conspiracy to commit murder.

Blake immediately posted Caldwell's one million dollar bail, which raised some eyebrows, but he would have to cool his heels in the county jail until March 13, 2003, when the judge finally set his bail at one and a half million dollars. The former television star was given strict bail requirements. He was forced to wear an ankle monitor and was not allowed to leave the state, which actually forced Blake to focus on his defense.

Blake hired high-profile attorney M. Gerald Swartzbach to lead his defense. Swartzbach had previously defended numerous leftist activists and indigent people on a pro-bono basis successfully and so gained quite a reputation in California as a capable defense attorney. After getting bail for Blake, Swartzbach began preparing his client's defense, which primarily involved shooting holes in what little evidence the prosecution had and calling the victim's character into question.

When the trial began in December 2004, the prosecution admittedly had an uphill battle.

The prosecution's case was that Blake wished to get out of the marriage with Bakley but retain custody of their daughter, which would have been voided under their prenuptial agreement if he initiated the divorce proceedings. As evidence, they pointed out that Bakley had her window rolled down, which they argued demonstrated that she knew her killer.

Although the murder weapon was found in a dumpster a few yards away, it had no fingerprints and could not be traced.

The prosecution had a difficult time showing the jury that Blake may have been the shooter since gunshot residue tests conducted on his hands the night of the murder came up negative. They were also never able to prove a definite conspiracy between Blake and Caldwell. The only payments that the prosecutors and police could uncover between Blake and Caldwell were for the normal salary the television star paid him for his bodyguard services.

It also did not help when a judge dismissed all charges against Caldwell.

With a case full of more holes than a slice of Swiss cheese, the prosecutors relied on their two "star" witnesses: Ronald "Duffy" Hambleton and Gary McLarty. Both Hambleton and McLarty, who were retired stuntmen, testified that Blake approached them at separate times to kill his wife. Their testimony was shaky at best and when Swartzbach cross-examined them, the two men looked like liars and opportunists.

Swartzbach was able to get both men to admit to heavy drug use and financial problems, and he also caught them in lies more than once. He asked both men why they did not immediately contact the police when approached with the murder for hire scheme. Neither man gave a credible answer. By the time Swartzbach was done cross-examining the former stuntmen, their testimony probably helped more than hurt Blake.

The final strategy employed by the defense was to call the character of Bonnie Bakley into question. The defense brought up the fact that this was Bakely's ninth marriage and that most of those marriages had ended acrimoniously. Swartzbach also painted Bakley as an unfit mother, a gold digger, and a con-woman. On the last point, he showed the jury Bakley's criminal record. Essentially, the defense argued that any number of former lovers and/or husbands of Bakley's may have been the murderer.

Although Blake never took the stand in his own defense, the

prosecution's case proved to be too weak for the jury to convict him, so on March 16, 2005, he was acquitted of the murder charge and one of the solicitation charges. The jury deadlocked on the other solicitation charge, which the judge then threw out.

Blake walked out of the courtroom a freeman, but because of the numerous unanswered questions surrounding the case, it is highly unlikely that the eighty-three-year-old actor will be given one last role before he dies.

CHAPTER 9:
The Cold Case Murder of Helen Sullivan

It has become increasingly difficult in recent years for murderers to hide their nefarious acts. Advances in forensic science have been at the vanguard of law enforcement's new tactics to solve old crimes. The national fingerprint database, AFIS, and the national DNA database, CODIS, have played a major role in the new fight to solve unsolved crimes. AFIS is a fingerprint database of all criminal offenders in the United States—misdemeanor and felony and CODIS is a DNA database of all offenders. The two databases began to be used nationwide in the 1990s and have been responsible for helping to solve hundreds of cold cases.

Beginning in the late 1990s, police departments around the United States began to form cold case squads in order to deal with the increasing back log of unsolved, or commonly referred to as "cold", murder and rape cases. Cold case squads are usually comprised of a combination of seasoned veterans who know the streets and younger detectives who have learned all the new forensic technologies and techniques while in college and at the police academy.

Often, cold case squads dedicate most of their resources to solving crimes in the more recent past because family members of the victim, as well as the perpetrator, are still alive. Solving such cases gives closure to victim's family and gets a murderer off the streets.

The most determined cold case investigators work on cases where nearly everyone involved has died.

Recently, the Long Beach, California, Police Department's cold case detectives solved a forty-year-old murder case, which was its oldest to date. Nearly everyone involved in the case died in the years following the horrific murder, but the investigators still solved the case through a combination of determination and advances in forensic science.

Today, Long Beach is a city of nearly half a million people, which makes it the second largest in Los Angeles County and the seventh most populous city in the state of California. From its early days, Long Beach was always much more blue-collar compared to Tinsletown just to the north, but in the first half of the twentieth century it became an affordable suburb for the throngs of Americans who migrated to California at that time. Unlike today, Long Beach until the 1980s enjoyed relatively low crime rates for a city its size and most of its neighborhoods were seen as desirable places to live until fairly recently.

A Horrible Discovery

January 21, 1972, was a cold evening in Long Beach. Edward Sullivan had just returned home from his graveyard shift job at the Shell Oil refinery. He expected to meet his wife, have breakfast with her, and then go to sleep as her day began.

But something was different when he entered his home.

The lights were all off as if no one was home. When he turned the lights on, he was gripped with terror to find the bloody, half nude body of his wife sprawled out on the floor. Beside himself, Edward managed all the strength he could to call the police. When the police arrived, they surveyed the scene and quickly came to the determination that Helen Sullivan was probably raped before she was murdered. The officers dutifully took biological samples from Helen, although with 1972 technology they could do no more than blood type the different samples. They stored the samples in the Long Beach Police Department's evidence locker where it would sit for over three decades.

In the meantime, the police investigating the case interviewed all the neighbors, who saw nothing, and dusted the Sullivan home for fingerprints, which also turned up nothing.

Since Edward was working all night, which was corroborated by dozens of people, he was quickly ruled out as a suspect.

But who would kill Helen Sullivan?

In 1972, Helen Sullivan was a fifty-eight-year-old mother of three adult daughters. By all accounts, Helen was a good neighbor, wife, and mother who had no enemies. To bring in extra money for the family, Helen worked as an Amway saleswoman.

Was her murder somehow related to her work?

The police did not think so and even told Helen's daughters years later that they thought the perpetrator was probably a career criminal who was either serving a lengthy sentence for a similar crime, or had been killed at the hands of the police or another criminal.

Other than that theory, though, the Long Beach Police had little with which to work.

A Cold Case Solved: Postmortem

As the 1970s moved into the 1980s, Edward Sullivan passed away and the three Sullivan daughters all married and started families of their own.

But the murder of their mother was never forgotten.

The Long Beach Police Department also did not forget. In the early 2000s, like many police departments around the United States, the Long Beach Police Department created its own Cold Case Squad in order to solve the growing backlog of unsolved murder cases.

It turns out that the effort to solve Helen Sullivan's murder was actually a race against time.

The Long Beach Police were destroying much of the older evidence in the storage locker to make room for newer cases. Lucky for the surviving members of Helen Sullivan's family, they had not yet got to 1972.

In 2012 the Long Beach Cold Case Squad received funding from the National Institute of Justice to clear its backlog of older cold cases. The National Institute of Justice is essentially the research arm of the Justice Department, which helps the various state, county, and local law enforcement agencies throughout the United States by providing money, advising, and occasionally manpower. When the Long Beach Cold Case Squad received money from the National Institute of Justice, they were able to run the biological samples taken from Helen Sullivan's body through the national DNA database known as CODIS.

A match was quickly made to a career criminal named Emanuel Miller, who was thirty-six years old at the time of Helen's murder. A quick look at Miller's record showed that Helen's murder was not the first or last crime he committed. Over the years, Miller had committed numerous sexual assaults, violent crimes, and property crimes. Essentially, Miller was a one man crime wave and it became clear to investigators that he was responsible for murder.

But why did he target Helen?

It turns out that Miller was recently paroled in January 1972 and that the parole system in California worked very differently then. When offenders were released from prison in 1972, there was little effort made by the Department of Corrections to track them the way they do today. Offenders were simply given some street clothes and a "gate fee" and then told to report to a parole officer within a few days. If the offender's sentence was complete, then he or she did not even need to report to a parole officer.

When Miller was released, he had no money or a place to go, so the police surmise that he was attracted to the many vacant homes in the Sullivan's neighborhood. The homes were vacant because the state of California was in the process of constructing the Artesia Freeway.

The match was good news for the Long Beach Cold Case Squad and the two living daughters of Helen Sullivan, but unfortunately Miller never faced justice for the crime because he died in 1990 at the age of fifty-six.

The Sullivan daughters, though, were grateful for the investigators efforts and glad to finally know who killed their mother.

"More people need to understand the good that comes out of getting final closure and that (cold case work) is one of the most important efforts out there today," Sullivan's daughter, Ann Luckey, then seventy-four, said. "Because it does help so many people."

Helen's youngest daughter, who was twenty-two at the time of the murder and sixty-two when DNA revealed the identity of the killer added.

"The good thing is DNA has proved who (the killer) is. If only they had it all those years ago, they could have maybe prevented other assaults."

CHAPTER 10:
A Guilty Conscience and the Cold Murder Case of Frederick Hart

As profiled and discussed in the last chapter, cold cases are often solved through a combination of science and good police work. The unfortunate reality is that anyone who can actually take the life of another human in cold blood usually has little to no remorse for what he or she has done. For most cold case killers, it is not the first crime they have committed, as many are seasoned criminals. They usually go to great lengths to conceal their crimes and rarely tell others about what they have done.

But sometimes, a killer has a conscience.

A Senseless Murder

In May 1990, Frederick Hart, known to his family and friends as "Ricky," was an average fifteen-year-old living in Galloway Township, New Jersey. Although located near Atlantic City and in Atlantic County, Galloway Township is a world away from the casinos, blight, and crime that have come to characterize Atlantic City.

Ricky was close to completing his freshman year of high school and looked forward to spending the summer with his family and friends. On the evening of May 7, Ricky had a fateful encounter with another area teenager.

Steven Goff, like Ricky Hart, grew up in New Jersey around Atlantic City. But unlike Hart, Goff was constantly in trouble with the law from an early age. Goff engaged in petty thefts, assaults, and drug use, which landed him in juvenile hall on more than one occasion. Goff's family could give him no direction and even if they could, the juvenile delinquent probably would not have listened.

On the evening of May 7, Goff's constant drug use and paranoia combined to lead him to murder Ricky Hart behind some condominiums in Galloway Township. When Ricky did not return home that evening, his parents called the police and filed a missing person report. The police and Ricky's friends and family scoured the area looking for the missing teen, but came up empty. Police interviews with Ricky's friends also turned up no leads.

The police could not say for sure if Ricky was a runaway or if he was abducted. The case was truly one of the biggest mysteries in the history of Galloway Township.

Then, about a year and a half after he disappeared, the decomposed corpse of Ricky Hart was discovered in a wooded area behind the condominiums. The autopsy of Ricky's remains quickly determined that he was never a run-away. He was murdered around the time he was reported missing and the cause of death was from multiple stab wounds.

Steven Goff had killed Ricky Hart, but he was not even on the list of potential suspects. The years would have to pass and Goff's guilty conscience would have to grow before this cold case could be solved.

A Troubled Life

In 2013, Steven Goff was a forty-one-year old man with a lot of demons in his closet. Not long after he killed Ricky, he was sent to state prison on drug charges. The stretch he did in prison in the early 1990s was not the first or last time that Goff would see the inside of a jail cell. As noted above, Goff had amassed a lengthy record as a juvenile and by 2013 he had eleven felony arrests and six convictions on his record.

The lengthy record meant that it was difficult for Goff to find well-paying and/or stable jobs. He tried various construction jobs and by 2013 was buying and selling stocks online, with which he found some success.

But those closest to Goff could see that he was in pain. Something was clearly bothering him.

In the years leading up to 2013, Goff moved into a home next to a man named Alan Rickel. Although Rickel was a few years older than Goff, the two became close friends. The two men would watch sporting events together and Rickel would sometimes hire Goff to work with him on construction jobs.

Then one day in early 2013, Goff gave a cryptic statement to Rickel.

"Al, you're not going to see me anymore." Goff told his friend. "I'm going to do something that will shock the world."

A couple of days later, Rickel went by Goff's house and was surprised to see that it looked like he had left. Goff's car was not in the driveway, his dog was nowhere to be found, and when he looked in the windows he noticed that many pieces of furniture were gone. Rickel wondered what happened to his troubled friend until he received a phone call from him a couple of days later. Goff said that he was near the Canadian border in Michigan, but that he was driving back to New Jersey to "meet his maker." Not knowing what Goff was talking about, but knowing that it was something big, Rickel wired his friend enough gas and toll money to get back to New Jersey.

The next call Rickel received was from deputies at the Atlantic County, New Jersey jail. They told him that Goff was being held on a murder charge and that he had requested Rickel to come pick up his car and dog.

Rickel was floored, but at the same time not all that surprised. He knew that his friend was hiding a big secret and apparently this is what it was.

Rickel later told reporters that he had an in-depth phone conversation with Goff, who was in jail, about the crime and the weight of his guilty conscience.

"He couldn't bear it anymore," Rickel said. "He told me he had nightmares. He'd go to sleep and see the kid's mother staring in his face."

Goff wanted to plead guilty at his first hearing, but the judge told him that it was only a formal reading of the charges.

The Guilty Plea

When Steven Goff finally pleaded guilty to Ricky Hart's murder in July 2013, a torrent of emotions was released by both him and Hart's family.

The Hart family also finally learned why Ricky was murdered.

Goff stated that he believed Ricky was going to testify against him on a burglary charge. The rest of the allocution consisted of statements of apology by Goff and victim impact statements by the Hart family.

"You deserve to see me suffer," said Goff to the Hart family. Goff then attempted to mitigate his crime to a degree.

"When we call him a child, we have to realize I was a child too. I just turned 18," Goff told Hart's tearful family. "I make no excuse for my action but I was strung out on drugs at the time… I wasn't in my right frame of mind."

For their part, the Hart family showed gratitude that Goff had finally come forward, but they stopped short of forgiveness.

"We're burying Freddie all over again," said Ricky Hart's uncle,

Gerald Tittermary Senior. Tiffermary's son then added, "Thanks for coming forward…I don't forgive you."

Goff was sentenced to thirty years behind bars and will have to serve at least fifteen years. Perhaps now Steven Goff will be able to forgive himself.

CHAPTER 11:
The Murder of Dominique Dunne

This book has profiled several high-profile crime cases and one, the Robert Blake case, where certain elements of it were a case of reality imitating art. The November 4, 1982, murder of Dominque Dunne was even more so a case of reality imitating art because the victim in this case was the daughter of a world renowned true crime author, Dominick Dunne.

The ironic murder of Dominque Dunne shocked the Hollywood community and proved to be fodder for a legion of true crime writers, including Dominick Dunne himself.

The case proves that no matter how much privilege and money someone may be born with, he or she can still end up a victim of domestic violence.

A Privileged Life

Dominique Dunne was born in 1959 to movie producer and true crime writer Dominick Dunne and his wife Ellen, who was a ranching heiress. Friends and extended family members of the Dunne's were involved in Hollywood and finance.

While growing up in southern California, Dominque went to the best schools that money could buy and lived for a while in Italy. Money was never a problem in the Dunne home and Dominque always wore the newest, trendiest clothes and drove expensive cars.

Truly, Dominque Dunne was born into a life of privilege.

Despite being born with a silver spoon, Dominque did not simply spend her family's money as some heirs are known to do, but instead parlayed her advantages into a lucrative acting career.

Using her family money, Dominque took acting lessons and then used her family connections to land small roles in television and film throughout the 1970s and into the early '80s. Her most notable role was as the eldest daughter of the beleaguered family in the 1982 feature film *Poltergeist*.

Besides the family connections that she inherited, Dunne was also born with natural beauty. The tall brunette often played guest star roles as a teenage love interest of one of the main characters and sometimes as an Italian, where she was able to showcase her knowledge of the Italian language and culture.

In 1981, the beautiful, accomplished, and cultured Dominque Dunne was on a trajectory course for success, which is why her friends and family were baffled when they learned she was dating John Sweeney.

The phrase "opposites attract" could not be truer in the coupling of Dominque Dunne and John Sweeney. The two met at a Los Angeles bar in 1981 and almost immediately became involved in a very physical yet tempestuous relationship.

John Sweeney came from humble origins and at the time that he began seeing Dominque, he was working as a restaurant cook. Although by most accounts Sweeney was a good cook and later became a professional chef, he had no real accomplishments to his name in 1981. Despite the difference in backgrounds, Sweeney was able to sweep Dunne off her feet and the two moved into a one bedroom apartment together in Hollywood just weeks after meeting each other.

From there the relationship went downhill.

According to Dunne's friends and family, Sweeney became abusive almost immediately after the two moved in together. Sweeney would regularly berate Dunne in front of their friends and Dunne later confessed that he hit her when no one was around.

After several rounds of counseling from friends and family, Dominque finally ended the relationship in September of 1982 and had the locks changed on the home they once shared.

John Sweeney was out of her life, or so she thought.

A Promising Life Cut Short

On the evening of November 4, 1982, John Sweeney was the last thing on Dominique Dunne's mind. Although Sweeney had left mental scars on Dunne with his abuse, the actress had moved on and on that night was rehearsing lines for her role in the upcoming miniseries *V* with actor David Packer. As the two were rehearsing their lines, their concentration was broken by a knock at the door.

It was John Sweeney.

At first, Dunne refused to speak with Sweeney, but he persisted and eventually she relented and went on the front porch to talk to him.

From that point, the details of the next several minutes remain murky because Packer stayed inside while Sweeney killed Dunne.

Packer later told police and testified in court that he heard the couple arguing and then what appeared to be a struggle and punching. He testified that he was afraid of Sweeney, so he did not immediately go outside and instead called the police who told him the address was out of their jurisdiction. Packer then called a friend and said that if he is killed that Sweeney is the culprit. Afraid, but seeing no other recourse, Packer then exited the home from a backdoor where he saw Sweeney on the side of the house standing over Dunne.

Sweeney told Packer that Dunne was dead and that he should call the police.

When the police arrived, Sweeney stated: "I killed my girlfriend and I tried to kill myself."

Dunne was brought to a local area hospital where she died days later as the result of oxygen deprivation inflicted when Sweeney strangled her. In a tragically ironic twist to the case, Dunne's last role was as an abuse victim on the police drama *Hillstreet Blues*. Since Dunne still had bruises on her arms from Sweeney's abuse, the directors of the show decided to film her with them for greater authenticity.

Dominque Dunne did not need to be a victim to play the part of a victim, but she was a victim.

The Trial of John Sweeney

After Dunne died as a result of the injuries she sustained from Sweeney's attack, he was charged with first degree murder. When Sweeney's trial began in 1983, there seemed to be little defense that he could offer for such a terrible crime. After all, he admitted to the assault and several witnesses could testify to the numerous bouts of domestic abuse he heaped on Dominique.

But attitudes were different in 1983.

"Domestic violence" had yet to become a phrase imbedded in the American lexicon as it is today and crime cases, even high-profile ones, were rarely tried in the media as they often are now. There was no World Wide Web, CNN was new and not available widely, and Court TV was still nearly a decade in the future, all of which were to the advantage of Sweeney.

Sweeney made the rare move of taking the stand in his own defense. He testified that he and Dominique had reconciled, but that she had suddenly changed her mind. The sudden change of heart by Dunne angered Sweeney, but he claims that he could not recall any of the details of the attack other than how he tried to revive her.

Essentially, the defense argued that Sweeney assaulted Dunne in the heat of passion and that it lacked forethought or malice and therefore the jury could not convict him of the most serious charges.

The prosecution hoped to put witnesses on the stand who would testify to Sweeney's abusive nature, thereby establishing a pattern of violence. The judge refused to allow the testimony of one of Sweeney's ex-girlfriends who claimed he didn't abuse her or any of Dominque's friends and family who claimed to have seen her after the bouts of abuse.

Clearly, things were very different in 1983.

The jury found Sweeney guilty of the lesser count of voluntary manslaughter on September 21, 1983. Sweeney was sentenced to six years in prison and served just over three before being paroled in 1986. After he was released from prison, Sweeney moved back to southern California where he landed a job as the head chef at an upscale restaurant. When the Dunne family learned of this development, they handed out flyers to the patrons that stated the head chef was a killer.

Sweeney eventually left California and changed his name.

Eventually, the Dunne family also moved on, but they never forgot about Dominique.

CHAPTER 12:
Eva Dugan and the Politics of Death

The preceding pages of this book deal primarily with deaths in one form or another, usually murders. Most the deaths profiled here brought unimaginable levels of grief to the loved ones of the deceased, but were quickly forgotten by most other people.

Unfortunately, death is a part of life and in today's society many of us have become de-sensitized to news stories about death.

But sometimes, death can lead to political changes.

The story of Jack Kevorkian, detailed earlier in this book, is one where the efforts by Kevorkian eventually led to changes in the "right to die" laws in some American states.

There are also numerous cases where political assassinations, most famously the murder of the archduke of Austria–Hungary in 1914, led to wars and other political changes.

Beyond these well-known cases, there are other cases where a death helped bring about changes in the laws. The 1930 execution of Eva Dugan in Arizona is one such case. Her execution brought the sometimes brutal realities of capital punishment to the forefront of the American news cycle and led to a change in the method of execution in the state of Arizona.

A Wild Life

Eva Dugan's early life is shrouded in mystery, but it is known that she was born in 1878, probably somewhere in the eastern United States. The attractive woman made her way to the northwest, like thousands of other people from around the world, to take part in the Klondike Gold Rush of the 1890s. The Klondike Gold Rush was similar to the earlier California Gold Rush in many ways in that it gave an economic boon to the region when thousands of people came to strike it rich. The Klondike Gold Rush saw over 100,000 people enter Canada's Yukon Territory in search of gold, but unlike in California, the Yukon rush was less sustained. Part of the problem was that the Yukon was much more isolated than California; the roads that connected it to Alaska and lower Canada can be described as poor at best and the first railroad was not completed until 1900.

A person had to have a combination of luck and toughness to make it during the Klondike Gold Rush.

Eva Dugan, like most involved in the Klondike, did not find gold and eventually ended up in Juneau, Alaska. It is known that she worked as a cabaret singer there and probably also as a prostitute. When the Gold Rush began to fizzle and most of the men began to move back south into the mainland of Canada and the United

States, Eva followed the men.

She eventually ended up in Tucson, Arizona.

Tucson in the 1920s was far different than it is today. Today, Tucson's inhabitants are a mixture of college students and retirees from the north, with a fairly large number of Hispanics. In 1920 Tucson was still a relatively small town with a frontier attitude.

It was precisely the type of town where Eva Dugan could fit in and take advantage of the situation. Women were in short supply in the Pima County/Tucson area, so any woman with marketable skills could be sure to find either work or a husband.

Although there were no cabarets in Tucson for Dugan to work in, there was a surplus of elderly men that needed attention. Some of these men desired wives to start families, while others wanted women for domestic household duties. Dugan came to Tucson to make money, not find a husband.

Eva Dugan had enough experience with marriage to last several lifetimes.

Later it was revealed that Dugan had been married five times before she arrived in Arizona. It was also learned that all five men had disappeared under mysterious circumstances. Along with her collection of ex-husbands, Dugan also had a daughter in White Plains, New York, which is probably where the cabaret singer grew up.

Eva Dugan spent a lifetime living off of men. Whether it was one of her husbands who vanished under mysterious circumstances or prospectors in Alaska and the Yukon Territory, Dugan knew how to manipulate men,

In the late 1920s, she set sights on a new target.

Another Mysterious Disappearance

Andrew Mathis was an elderly rancher who had amassed a small fortune buying and selling chickens in Pima County. Mathis hired the aging Dugan to take care of the domestic duties in his home: cooking, cleaning, and running various errands for the rancher. Dugan seemed to have found a home and legitimate work.

The problem was, she was terrible at the job.

After numerous arguments about the quality of her work, Mathis fired Dugan and told her to pack her things. Not long after Dugan was terminated from her job, Mathis, like Eva's five husbands, disappeared mysteriously.

The Pima County authorities became suspicious when the popular rancher was nowhere to be found and their suspicions were heightened when Dugan also appeared to be missing.

What happened to rancher and his maid?

Today, it is easy for the authorities to locate a person who is "on the grid." If the person in question uses a credit card or withdraws money from his or her bank account, then the authorities can know almost instantly where that person is.

In the late 1920s, the police had to wait for the person in question to make a mistake.

Eva Dugan's mistake was her greed. She sold Mathis' Dodge coupe in Kansas City, which put the authorities on her tail and led to her arrest in White Plains, New York. Believing that Dugan was much more than just a car thief, the Pima County authorities filed formal extradition papers and once granted by a judge in New York, they traveled to New York and brought her back to Arizona.

Dugan was quickly convicted of auto theft in Pima County and imprisoned in the county jail for nine months; but while the femme fatal cooled her heels in county, the local police were searching frantically for Andrew Mathis.

The deserts of southern Arizona are a vast and foreboding place and any corpse hidden there is often quickly destroyed by coyotes and other animals, not to mention the heat. A clever criminal would have buried Mathis' body far away from any roads or dwellings, but Dugan instead chose to bury the corpse on his own land.

Perhaps she was unable to carry the body very far because of her advanced age, or possibly the fact that she had gotten away with five prior murders gave her a sense of overconfidence in her criminal abilities. Whichever was the case, the local police discovered Mathis' remains in a shallow grave.

Eva Dugan was promptly charged with Andrew Mathis' murder.

Dugan's trial was short and although the prosecution's evidence against her was entirely circumstantial, it was convincing. The prosecutor showed the jury how Eva disappeared with Mathis' car shortly after he went missing. The judge also allowed the prosecution to show the jury that Dugan's five ex-husbands had also disappeared under mysterious circumstances. The jury did not take long to return a guilty verdict and with it the death penalty.

Eva Dugan gave a defiant statement to the jury before she was brought to the prison in Florence to await her sentence.

"Well, I'll die with my boots on, an' in full health," said Dugan to the jury. "An' that's more'n most of you old coots'll be able to boast on."

An Execution that Changed the Law

Instead of spending her time with legal maneuvers or finding god, as many death row inmates do today, Eva Dugan decided to cash in on her status as one of the only death row inmates in America. She agreed to give interviews to any media outlet, as long as they paid her one dollar per interview.

But as the doomsday approached, Eva Dugan decided to take matters into her own hands.

On the day before her scheduled execution, the guards at the prison searched Dugan's cell and found a bottle of ammonia and some razor blades. Although she did file a last minute appeal on the ground that she was mentally ill, Eva Dugan went to the gallows were her head held high. According to one news report she told the executioners, "Don't hold my arms so tight, the people will think I'm afraid."

On February 21, 1930, Eva Dugan became the first woman executed in the state of Arizona.

Besides the macabre glass ceiling that Dugan broke for the female criminals of the Grand Canyon state, her execution was botched, which led to changes in the Arizona laws pertaining to the method of execution.

Since Dugan was the first woman to be executed in Arizona and she made herself into somewhat of a media celebrity, throngs of reporters were there to see her executed—and to watch as her body was dismembered.

Although Dugan was already dead by the time her head became detached from her body, the grisly scene was too much for Arizona lawmakers. The method of execution in Arizona was legally changed from hanging to the gas chamber in 1934.

After a life of scams and murder, Eva Dugan's death proved to be the catalyst for change.

Conclusion

Crime is a terrible thing, but there is no mistaking that some crimes are so astonishing that their story needs to be told. As humans, we can learn a lot about the frailties of the human condition by examining some of the most astonishing crimes in our history. The examination demonstrates that people from all walks of life and all socioeconomic classes, can possibly become the victims of a serious crime.

The examination also shows that there are people from all backgrounds who can and do commit these astonishing crimes.

The twelve cases profiled in this book graphically depict how serious crimes can happen to anyone and come from anywhere.

More books by Jack Rosewood

SAVE $32 by getting this boxed set of eight (8) books instead of buying them one by one!

- Cousins David Alan Gore and Fred Waterfield, who found at an early age that both shared sick sexual fantasies of rape and murder and sought out victims to fulfill those fantasies;
- Australian serial killer Eric Edgar Cooke, who selected his victims and his methods of murder at random, shooting some, stabbing others, until he was finally hanged, the last man to face the gallows in Perth;
- William Heirens, who went from being the most popular boy in his class to a murderer who was completely out of a

control, even going so far as to leave a desperate message at one scene, written in lipstick: "For heavens sake catch me before I kill more. I cannot control myself";
- Belle Gunness, a stocky Norwegian woman who cold-bloodedly killed several of her children, husbands and suitors in order to obtain their life insurance policies and cash – or eliminate witnesses, burying most in wooden trunks beneath the hog pen;
- Joseph Paul Franklin, who confessed to the attempted murder of Hustler magazine publisher Larry Flynt and killed multiple others – most often interracial couples - as his own personal form of "racial cleansing," inspired by reading Hitler's "Mein Kampf";
- John Christie, a slender but sadistic killer whose British flat was found stuffed with dead bodies including that of his own wife, who was discovered buried beneath the floorboards, when he was finally arrested in 1950s;
- Patrick Wayne Kearney, who killed young men hitching through California in the 1970s, usually with a bullet to the back of the head, then had sex with their dead bodies; and
- Jerry Brudos, who sadistically murdered several young women after torturing them in his family's garage, saving ghoulish mementos including a foot he kept in the freezer, which he brought out like a toy in order to display it in stolen high heels, masturbating from the sheer pleasure of it all.

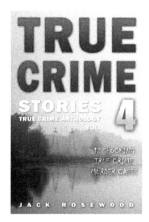

WARNING! The following true crime book may shock and frighten the faint hearted. In the pages of this book are assembled twelve of the strangest true crime stories in human history. There is no doubt that some of these cases will disturb you, but it is equally assured that you will not be able to put this book down!

Follow along in various criminal investigations as astute investigators race to solve cold murder cases. Some of the cases in this true crime anthology will boggle your mind as much as the police were when they investigated them. You will read about the abduction of girls from safe neighborhoods during broad daylight and how the dogged detectives eventually caught their killers through a combination of advances in science, some lucky breaks, and excellent police work. There are also some true crime murder cases profiled where killers have yet to be brought to justice and unfortunately, probably never will be. You may have already heard about some of these cases, while it will be the first time you read about others, but make no mistake, you will keep turning the pages for more.

So open the pages and read about bizarre abductions, true murder cases, and other strange crimes that have intrigued people around the world. Once you do, you will want to read more.

GET THESE BOOKS FOR FREE

Go to www.jackrosewood.com

and get these E-Books for free!

A Note From The Author

Hello, this is Jack Rosewood. Thank you for reading this book. I hope you enjoyed the read. If you did, I'd appreciate if you would take a few moments to post a review on Amazon.

I would also love if you'd sign up to my newsletter to receive updates on new releases, promotions and a FREE copy of my Herbert Mullin E-Book, visit www.jackrosewood.com

Thanks again for reading this book, make sure to follow me on Facebook.

Best Regards

Jack Rosewood

CPSIA information can be obtained
at www.ICGtesting.com
Printed in the USA
LVHW051616260420
654441LV00016B/2857